(UN)IMAGINABLE

The Pandemic Series

MELISSA DINWOODIE

(UN)Imaginable

tellwell

Tellwell Talent
www.tellwell.ca

ISBN
978-0-2288-3425-0 (Hardcover)
978-0-2288-3423-6 (Paperback)
978-0-2288-3424-3 (eBook)

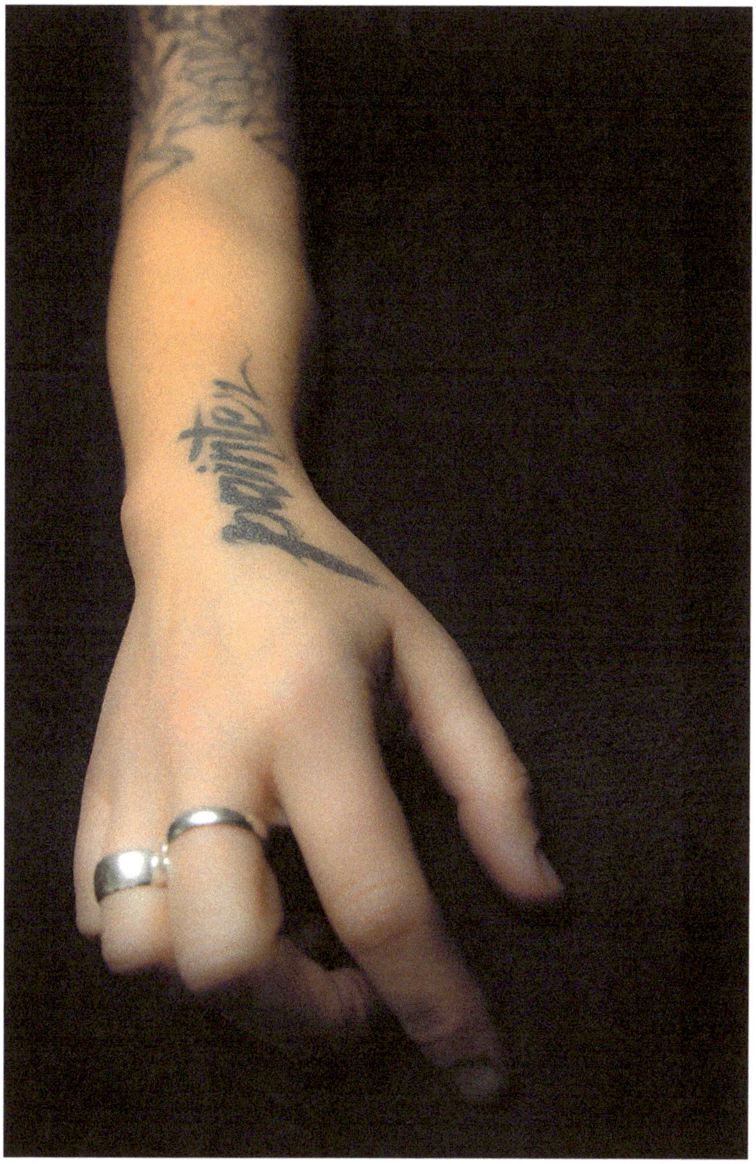
painter

DEDICATION

For everyone searching for a way to connect.
For all the artists that feel the most alive when alone, practicing their art.

But mostly for my parents, who have always supported my
dreams and inspire me to be better every day.

60 DAYS. 60 PAINTINGS.

INTRODUCTION

The Pandemic Series
March 28 - May 26, 2020

This series, aptly named *Pandemic*, started exactly 10 days after I was laid off from my day job, due to the COVID-19 pandemic. I think I took the first 10 days to be in denial over what was happening and in disbelief that it could actually happen. After the new reality settled into my mind, I decided that I was going to use this time that I had been "given" to paint full-time. I publicly declared, through social media, that I would paint one piece a day, every day, until all this was over. Knowing now, that in some ways it will never be over, I had to come up with a different end date, as I had no intention of creating a never-ending series. I went back to my day job on May 22, which was #56 in the series, so I decided that #60 would be a nice number to end on.

Every morning, I would have coffee and write. I would write about how I was feeling that day, or what I was thinking about or emotionally reacting to, from the media or a phone conversation. This would usually give me a starting point for that day's painting. A word or theme or feeling would emerge, and I would then move into my studio. This series allowed me to be free and expressive in my process, as each piece didn't have to relate to one another, the only common thread being that they were created during the time of self-isolation from the virus.

I posted each painting every day on social media, and wrote a bit about my day and my thoughts to go along with each one. As the series grew, the response from people online was humbling, rewarding and completely unexpected. What started as a project to keep myself busy became something so much bigger than the original idea, and way grander than myself. It evolved as the days passed by, and it became more than just a creative outlet for myself, but a way to navigate through the confusion and craziness of unprecedented times.

I am so grateful for the desire and need to create—although some days were harder than others—and this series carried me through a time that would've been difficult without it.

#1

TIME

MARCH 28, 2020

This is the first piece in my *Pandemic* series (a word we're all too familiar with now). I was writing my daily morning pages today & the word that kept coming to me was TIME. Even though this is such a strange thing we are all going through, I realized that I have been given the gift of time. Usually I'm in a rush, for work, appointments, meeting someone, household stuff, etc., but right now I have time. Time to take my time. So for this series, I'm going to let myself explore & experiment in my art (& life). I'll let myself play & make marks on the paper & see what happens. I'm grateful for TIME!

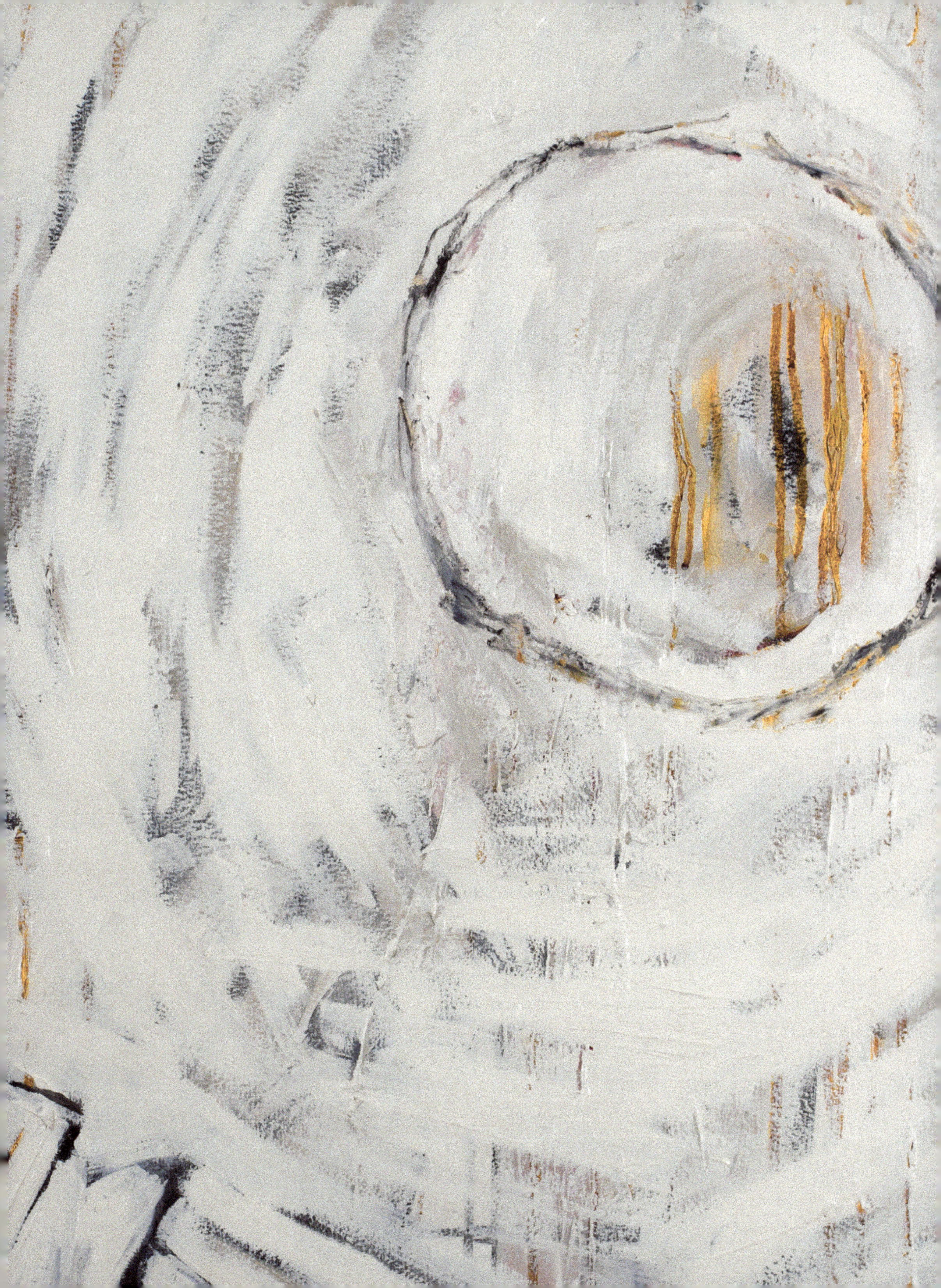

#2

GRASPING

MARCH 29, 2020

I had to grasp today. . . with several different thoughts/feelings. Talking to people with so many opinions on this global situation made me grasp for my own clear, unobstructed viewpoint. . . grasp to find the motivation to get into my studio (which hardly ever happens, but today was a weird one for me) . . . grasp at the fact that the only thing we know for sure is that we don't know when all this will end. Stay connected & tell your people you love them.

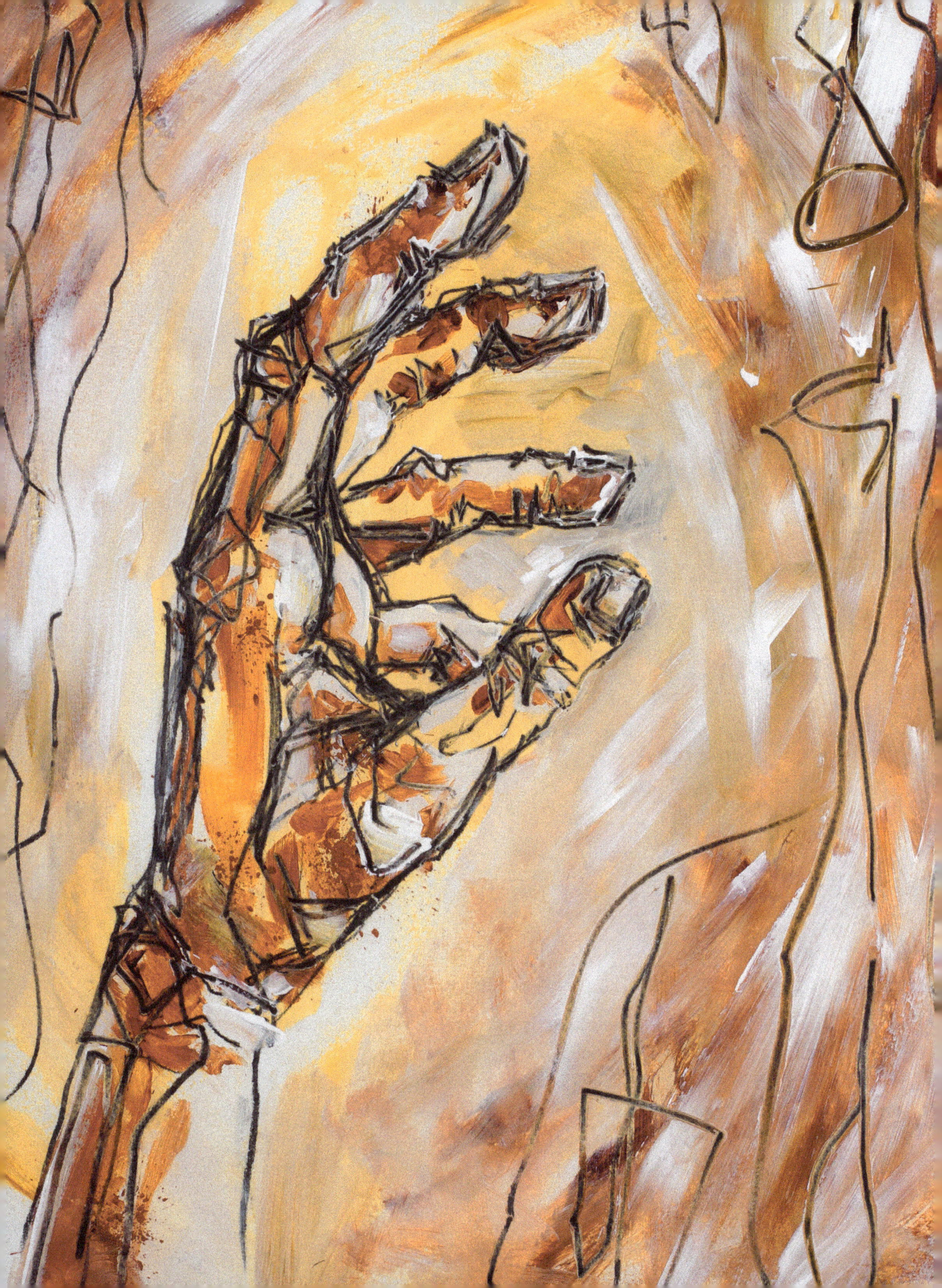

#3 CONNECTION

MARCH 30, 2020

While I was writing & reflecting this morning, I realized that while we are all missing our people, it seems that we are putting extra effort into connection & connecting with people more often than we would in normal circumstances, with phone & video calls, messages & comments. I've had & heard of so many connections that would've never happened pre-virus. So, while we are all missing the physical connection, let's all be grateful we are able to connect in other ways right now.

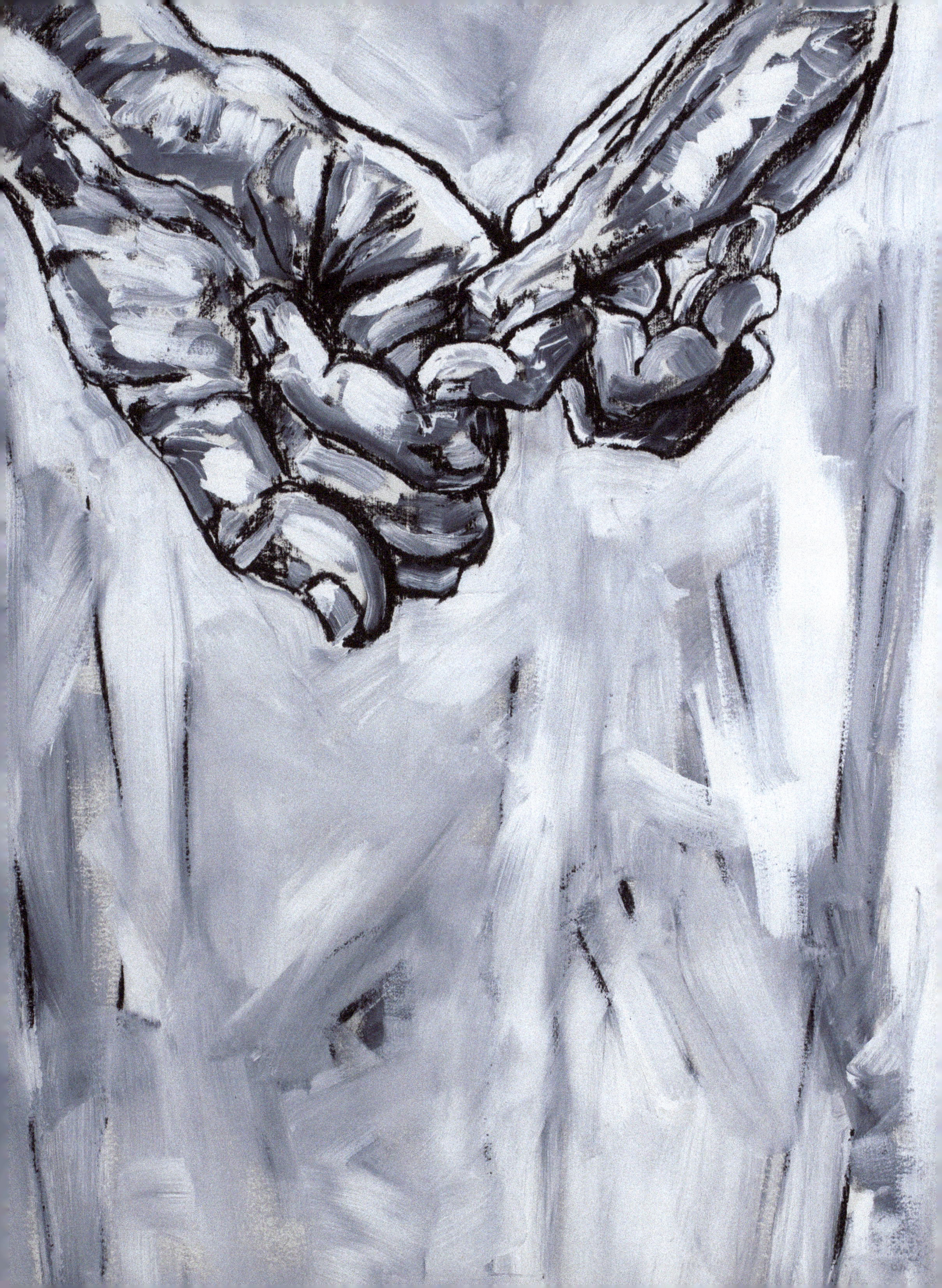

#4
GRATEFUL
MARCH 31, 2020

So many things to be grateful for (while of course there's anxiety & financial worries) I realize that I'm so fortunate in so many ways—living where I do, surrounded by beauty, having the technology that we do to connect with my people—having the time & ability to work on my art, on myself & to grow & learn & just be. Now don't get me wrong, there's a fair share of Netflix happening too (LOL), but with all that's going on, I'm grateful. And it's the things I am grateful for that I'm directing my energy toward.

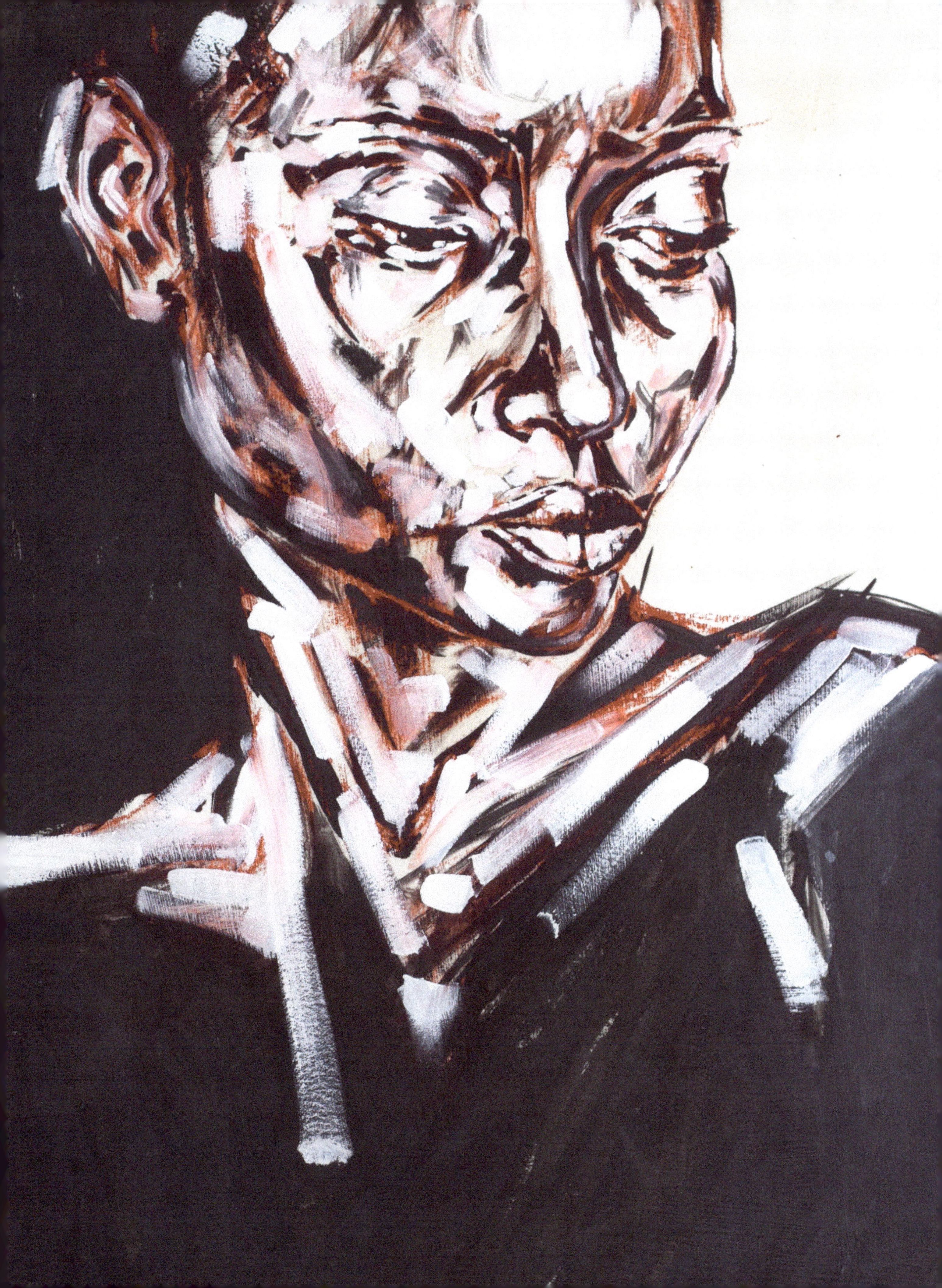

#5

NORMAL

APRIL 1, 2020

I went for a walk this morning, which felt normal, but then didn't really because there were no other people around. Is this our new normal? Do we really want our old normal? Aspects of it, yes, of course. Maybe we'll create a new, better normal. Just some random thoughts I was having. I'm so grateful for my studio, because when I'm in there, I feel like me. Creating feels normal. Do what makes you happy.

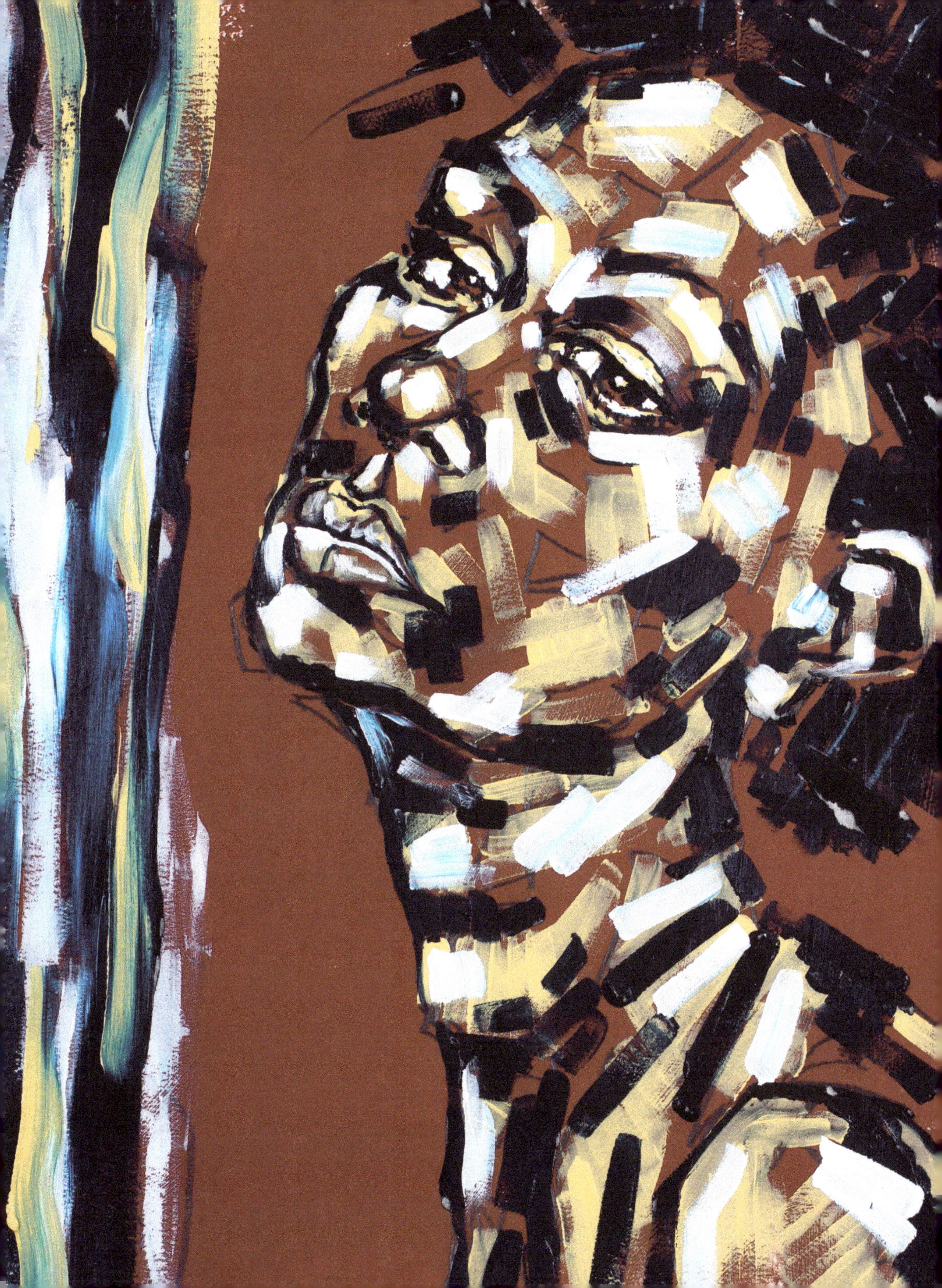

#6

WEIRD

APRIL 2, 2020

I've been saying this word a lot lately. . . weird. Everything seems weird—little things, day-to-day things, big things. I've never been one to shy away from weird, so I'll embrace this weirdness & use it. I definitely put it into this piece. . .

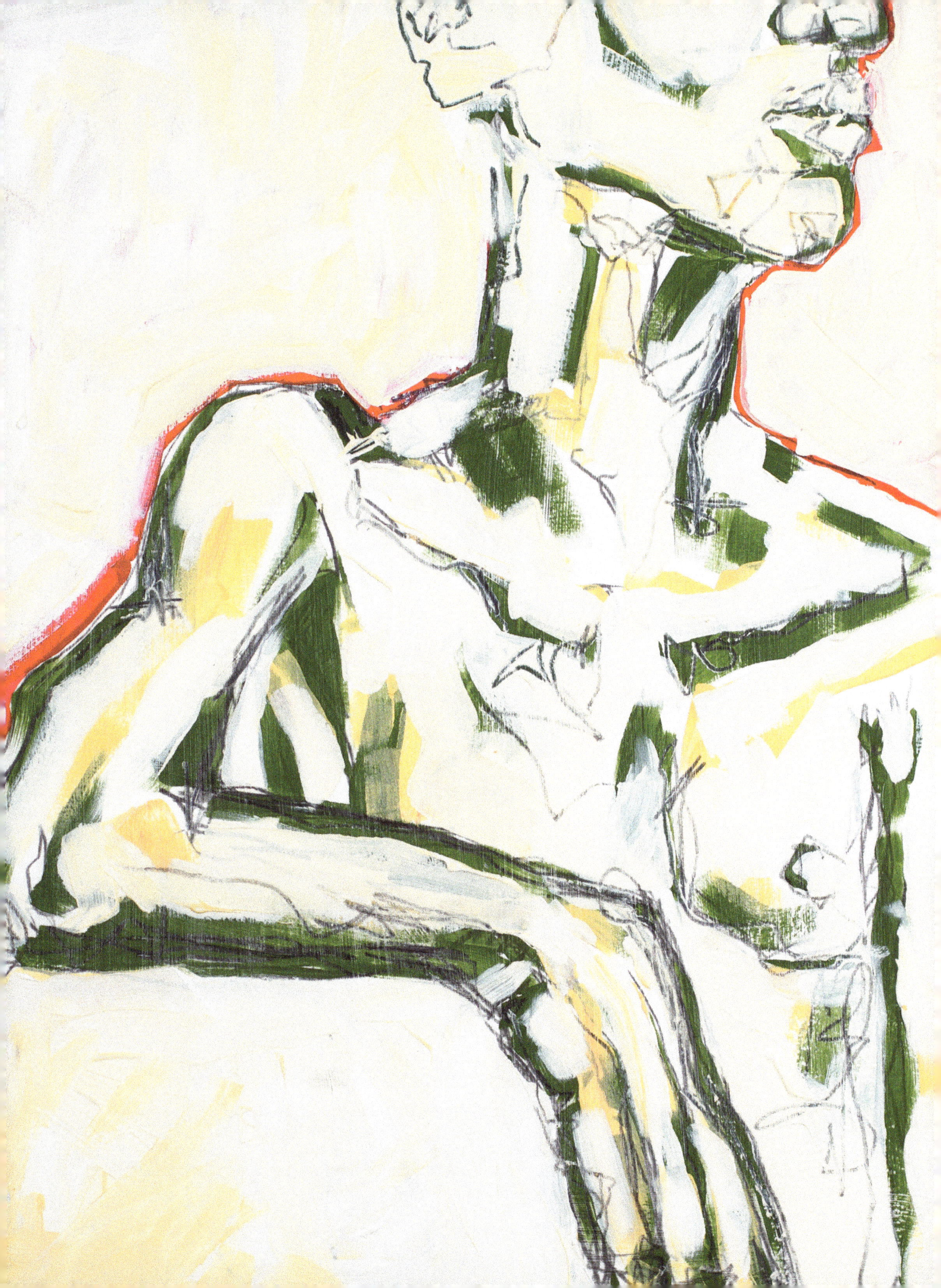

#7

VULNERABLE

APRIL 3, 2020

We're probably all feeling a little vulnerable right now—I know I am—but I'm not sure that's a negative thing. I think if we let ourselves be vulnerable, we let go of a lot of things that might've been dragging us down before, opening ourselves up to different possibilities. This is one of the very few self-portraits I've ever done. Feeling vulnerable.

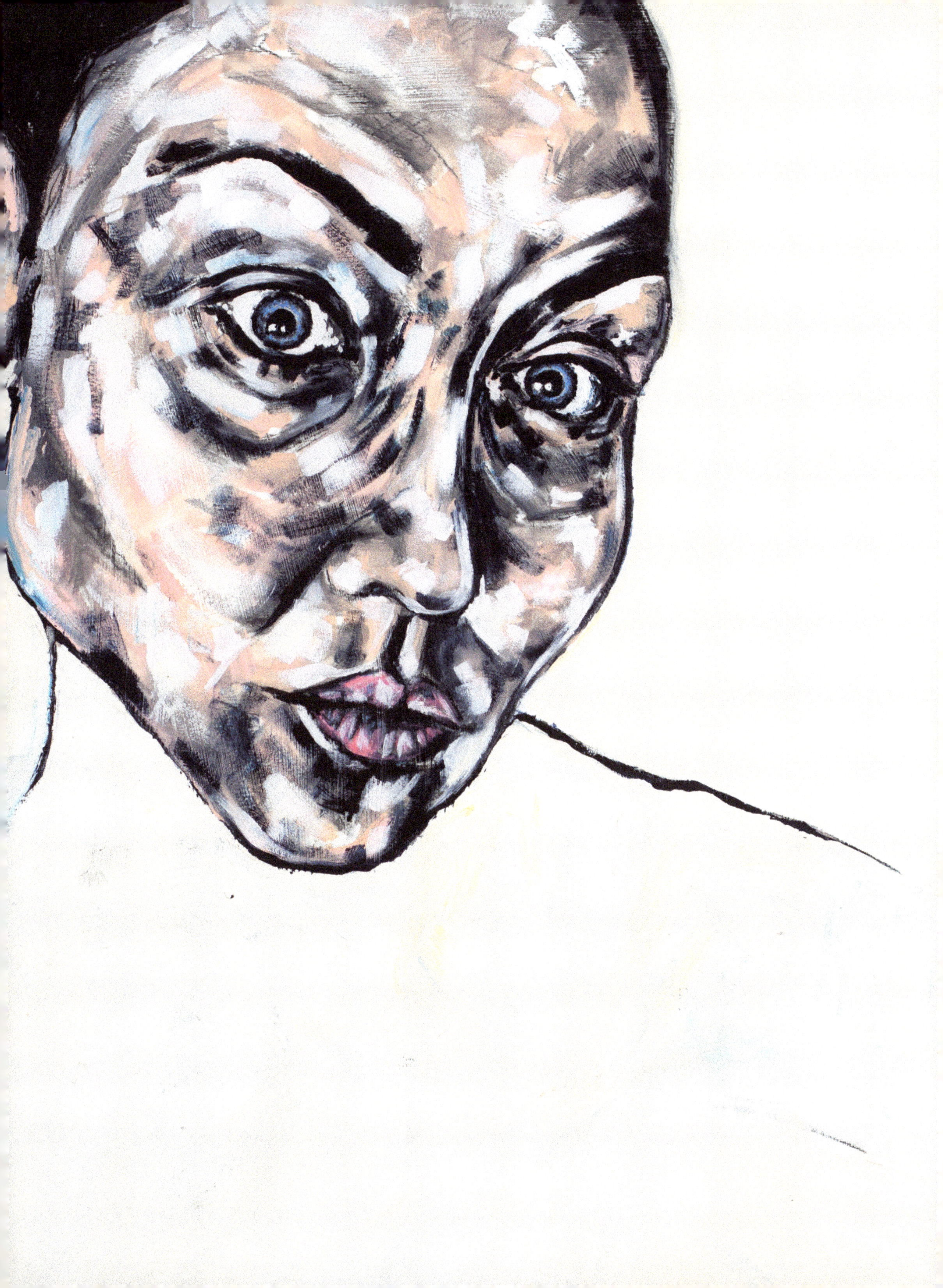

#8

LETTING GO

APRIL 4, 2020

While I was writing this morning, I was thinking about how we've all been letting go of so much—things, activities, day-to-day stuff. Some things we'll go back to & maybe some we won't, but we are practicing & achieving "letting go." Although it's not easy, it's a positive practice—letting go of control. With this series that I'm doing, I feel as though I'm letting go of what I thought my art should look like & just letting it happen. . . it's a very free feeling. . . letting go.

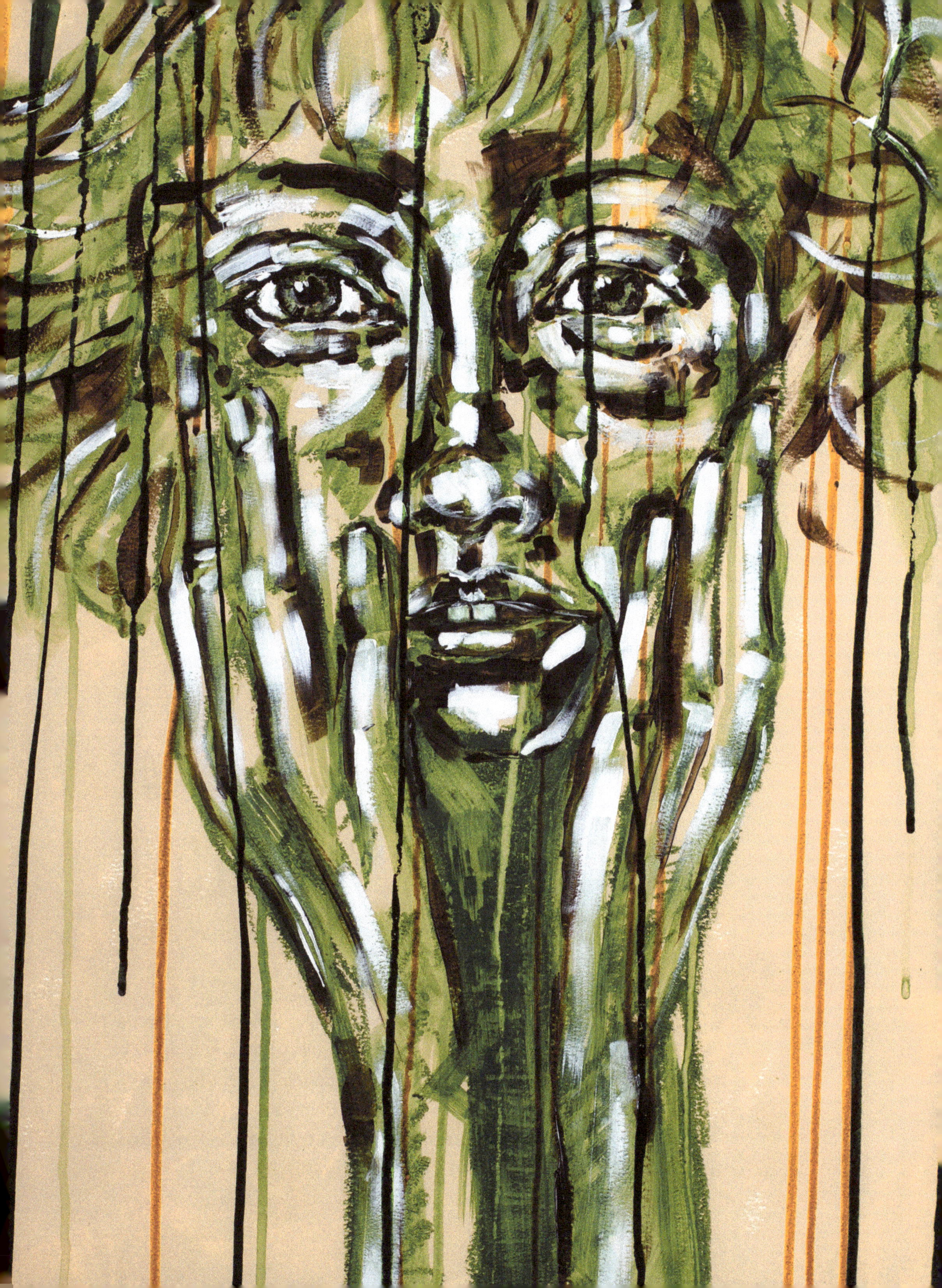

#9

ALONE

APRIL 5, 2020

Being alone is different than being lonely, but sometimes it's difficult to separate the two. Living alone during this crazy time, well. . . it has its challenges. There are glimpses of the lonely, but being alone is the constant—no sounding board, no outside distractions—only yourself & your own thoughts & actions. Being alone, you can learn a lot about the relationship you have with yourself & then work on it. So, while I have no other choice, I will cherish being alone & learn a thing or two while I'm at it.

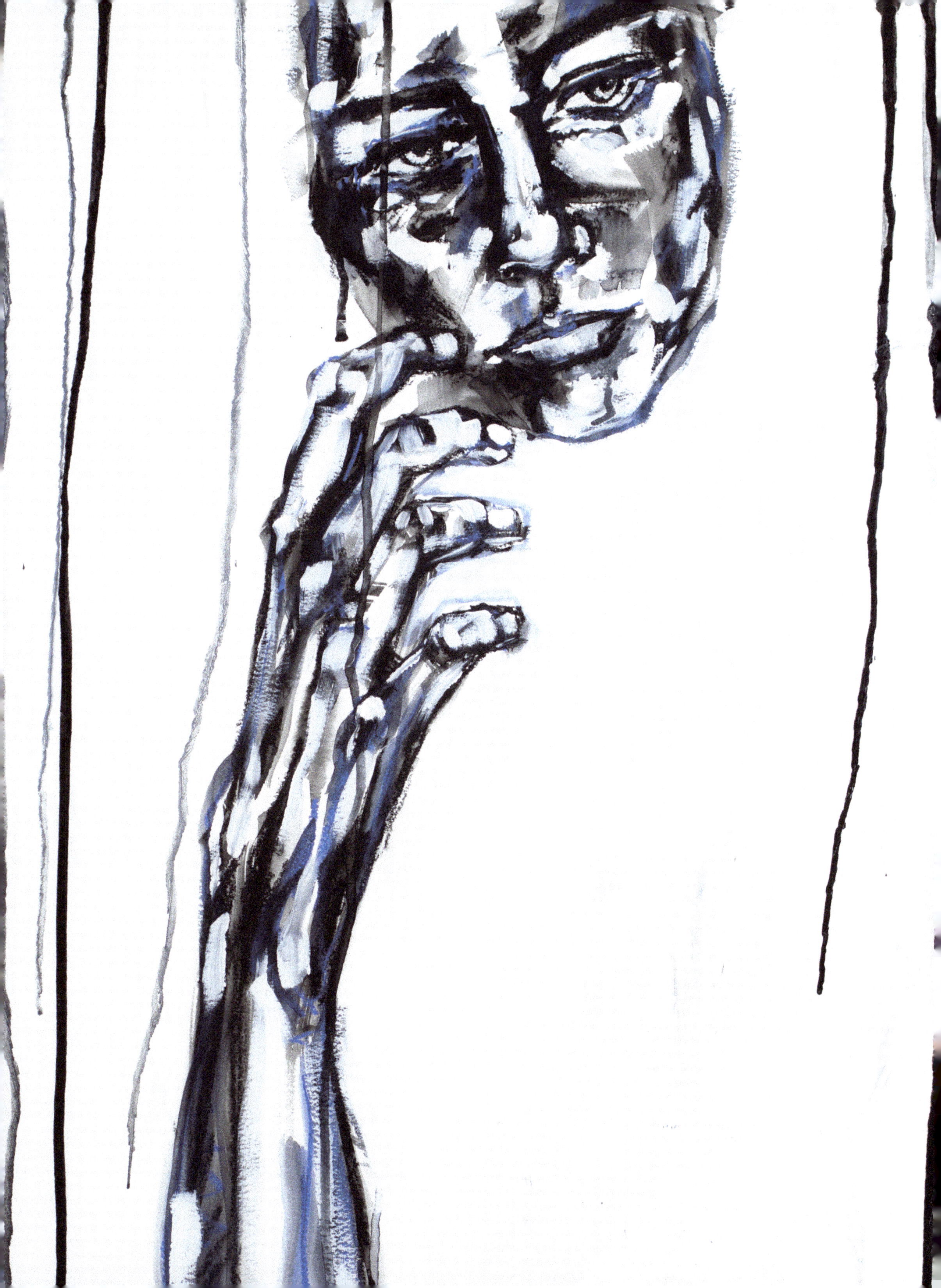

#10
UNCERTAINTY
APRIL 6, 2020

I am absolutely certain that we all are feeling bits (or SO MUCH) of uncertainty these days—so many questions, so few answers of certainty. How much certainty did we have in our lives before? It felt like we did, but we never knew what life would bring on any given day. I mean, when we really think about it, the only thing we can be certain of right now is this very moment. Whether we have to stay home or not, this is the moment we can be certain about. Do what makes you happy, challenge yourself & don't let fear stop you from owning this moment. All I have is right now & I am going to LIVE IT.

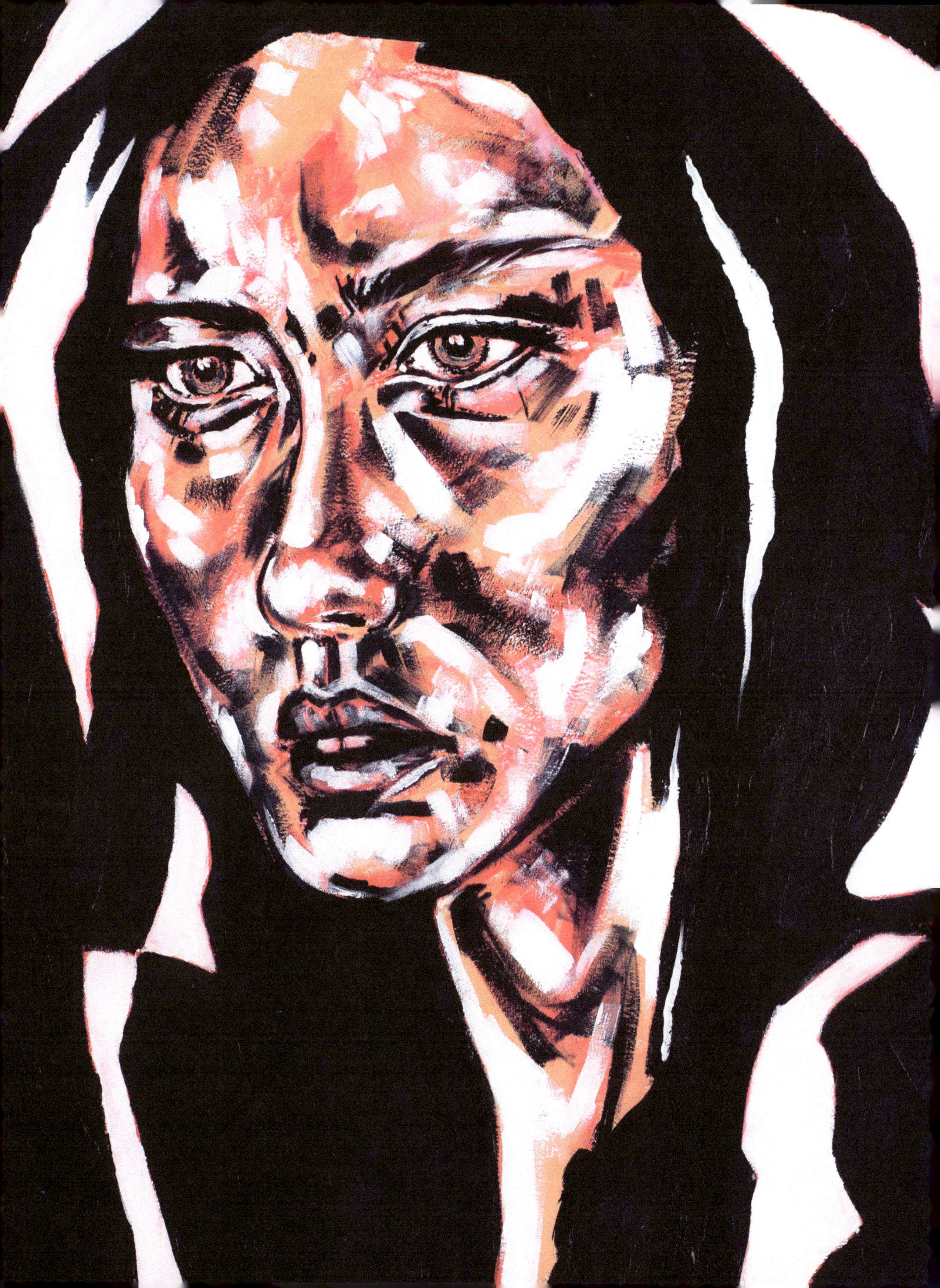

#11

FEEL

APRIL 7, 2020

So much to feel these days. I was contemplating that what we feel can drive us, point us in the direction we need to go. Even the negative feelings, we can use them as fuel to charge through this, so that when we get to the other side, we're stronger than we were before. We won't let them push us down, but rather use them to make us better. Feel them all, every single emotion, & then decide how you want to use them.

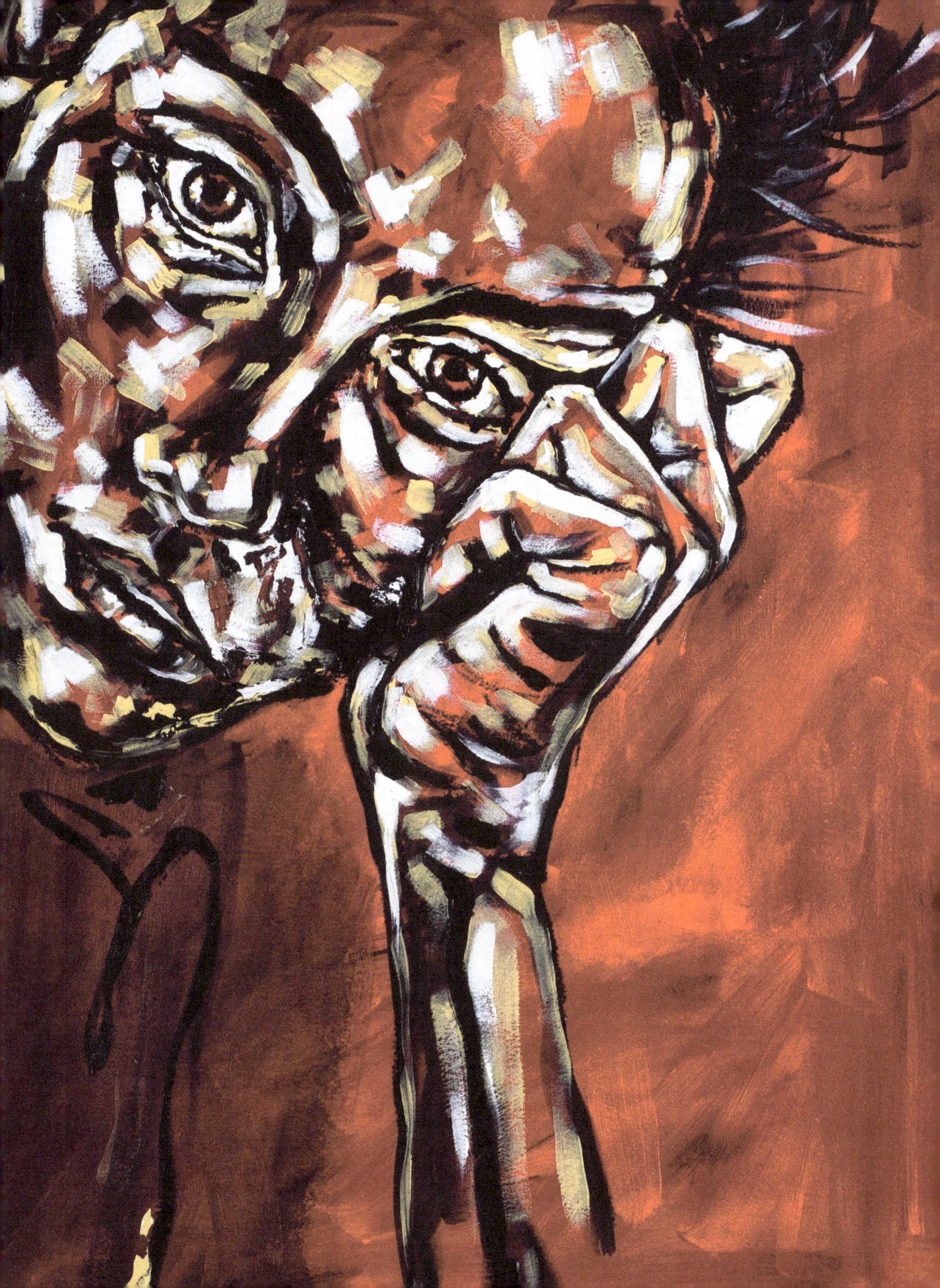

#12

HOPE

APRIL 8, 2020

Waking up today, I was so grateful for the sunshine—I mean really happy about it. I think the warmth of the sun is the feeling of hope. Hope is what gets us through tough times, it's what we hold onto as we move forward, it's that sparkle inside of you that beams out your eyes. I'm going to soak up as much sunshine as possible & not lose hope.

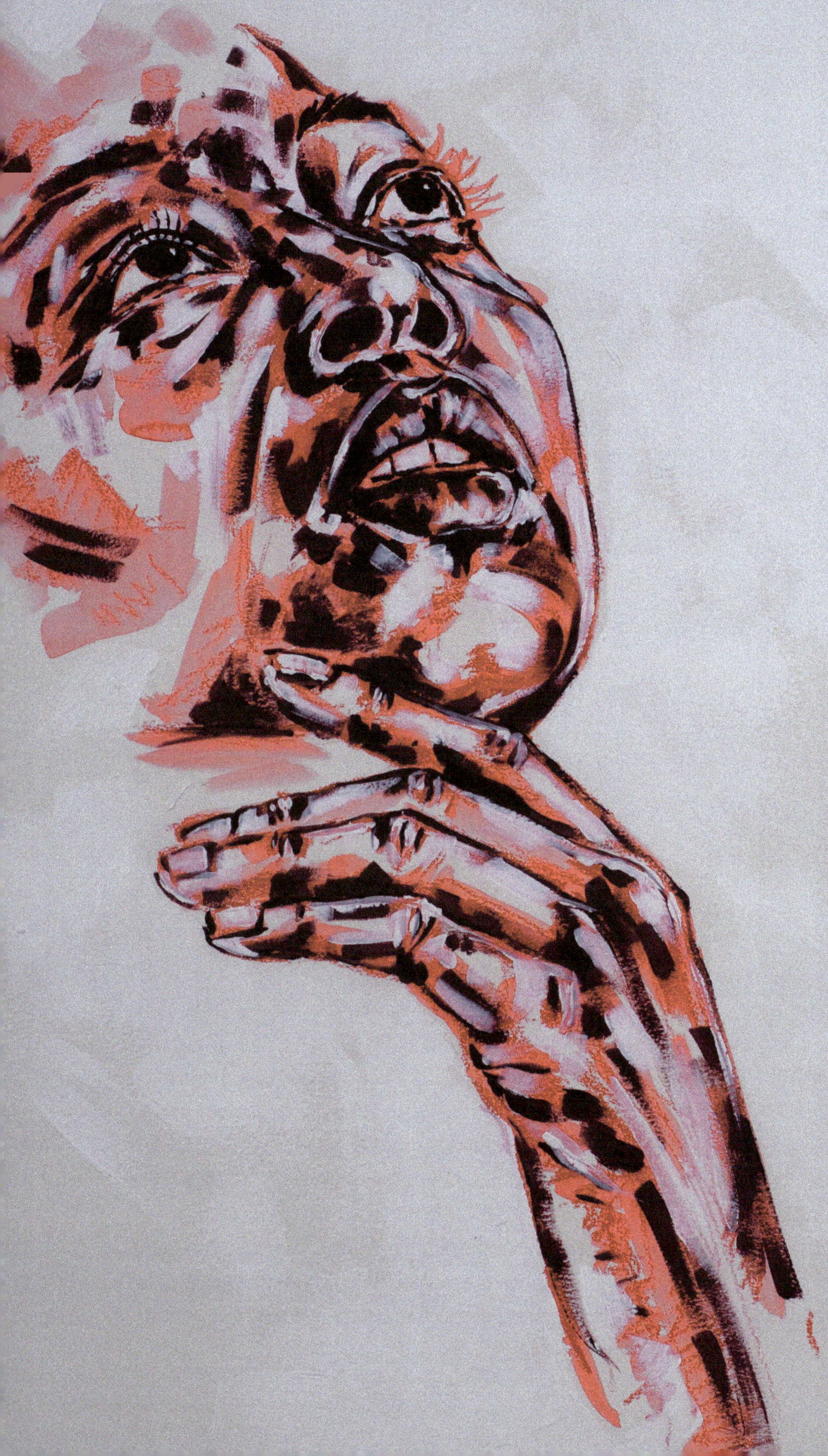

#13

FRUSTRATION

APRIL 9, 2020

Even while posting this I am filled with frustration—which I know we all have been feeling lately with all our emotions coming in waves. We want answers that can't be given. Today though, I had to call Service Canada because they needed more info to process my claim, & really needing the money, I waited on hold, & waited. In my 5th HOUR of waiting I started to paint this, & then finally after 6 hours they picked up only to tell me it was the wrong department & no, they could NOT transfer me. I had to call a different number, which I am currently on hold with. . . frustrated, helpless, annoyed. I know this is actually a small thing & we are all having our moments. I will do my very best to let myself feel the frustration but not let it take hold of me. Tomorrow is a new day.

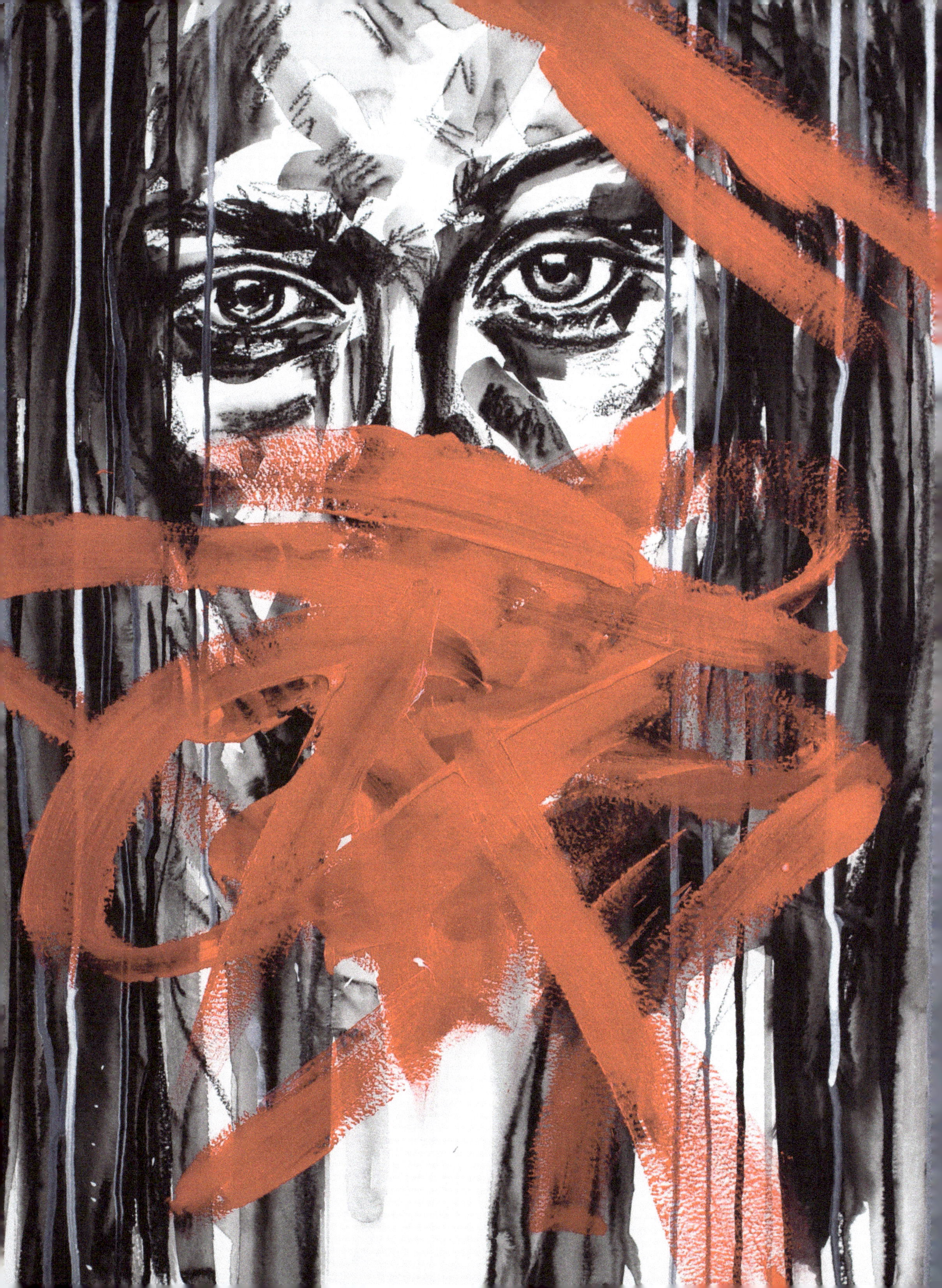

#14

ADAPT

APRIL 10, 2020

Different thoughts about this situation come at different times. Making sense of it all is a bit moot, but I don't think we need to. We (us humans & all creatures really) are adaptable— crazy, amazingly adaptable—& while the thought of adapting to all this may make you cringe, we're already doing it every day. It's in us. We have to roll with it, it's all about moving forward, to great heights. We will adapt.

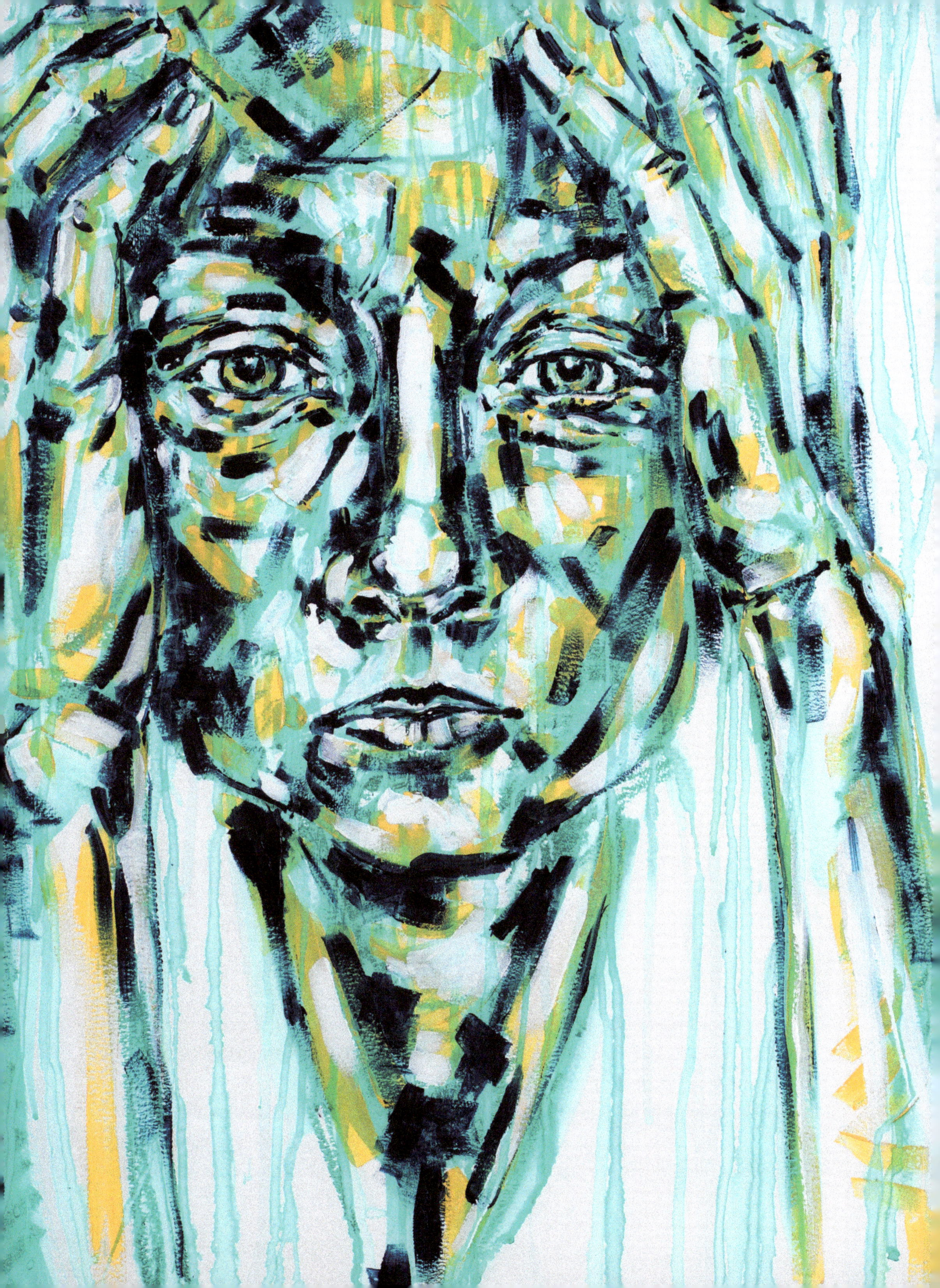

#15

PURPOSE

APRIL 11, 2020

Waking up with purpose—it's a necessity I think, at least for me & my wellbeing. Losing your job will take the initial purpose out of you real quick. It's an unsettling feeling. I'm grateful that I've developed some kind of routine to my day since all this happened & realized how important it is to get up & have purpose & intent—whatever that means to you—one thing that fills you with accomplishment & makes you feel like YOU. My art does that for me. It's my daily practice & my life's purpose... find yours & do it with intent.

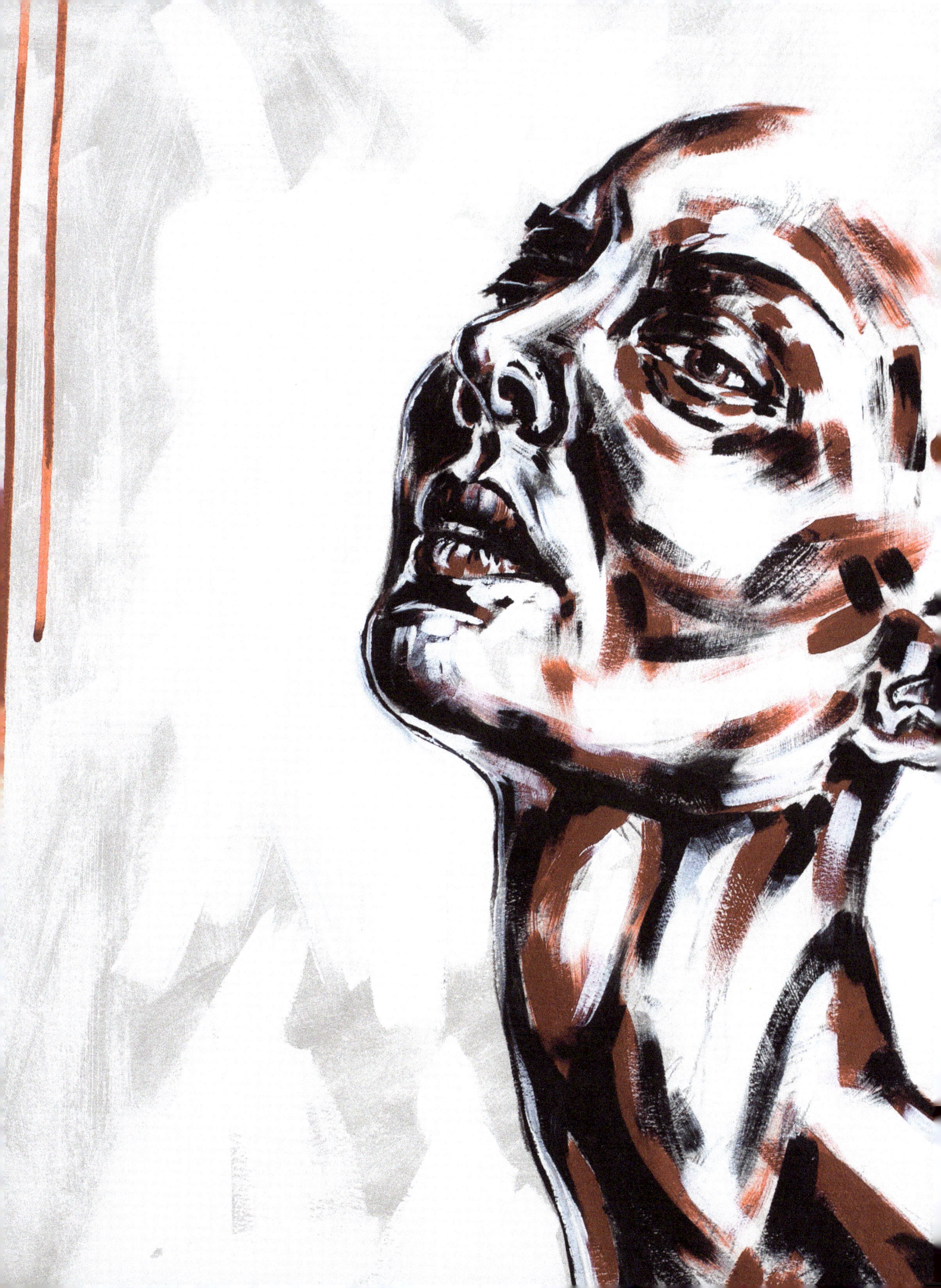

#16

REFLECT

APRIL 12, 2020

Today feels quiet. A day usually spent with family is a day I'm now using to reflect. No monumental brainstorming, but letting all the little ideas, memories, mistakes & triumphs just linger. We've all gone through so much in our lives, with so many experiences. Take a minute to reflect & notice how amazing we all are.

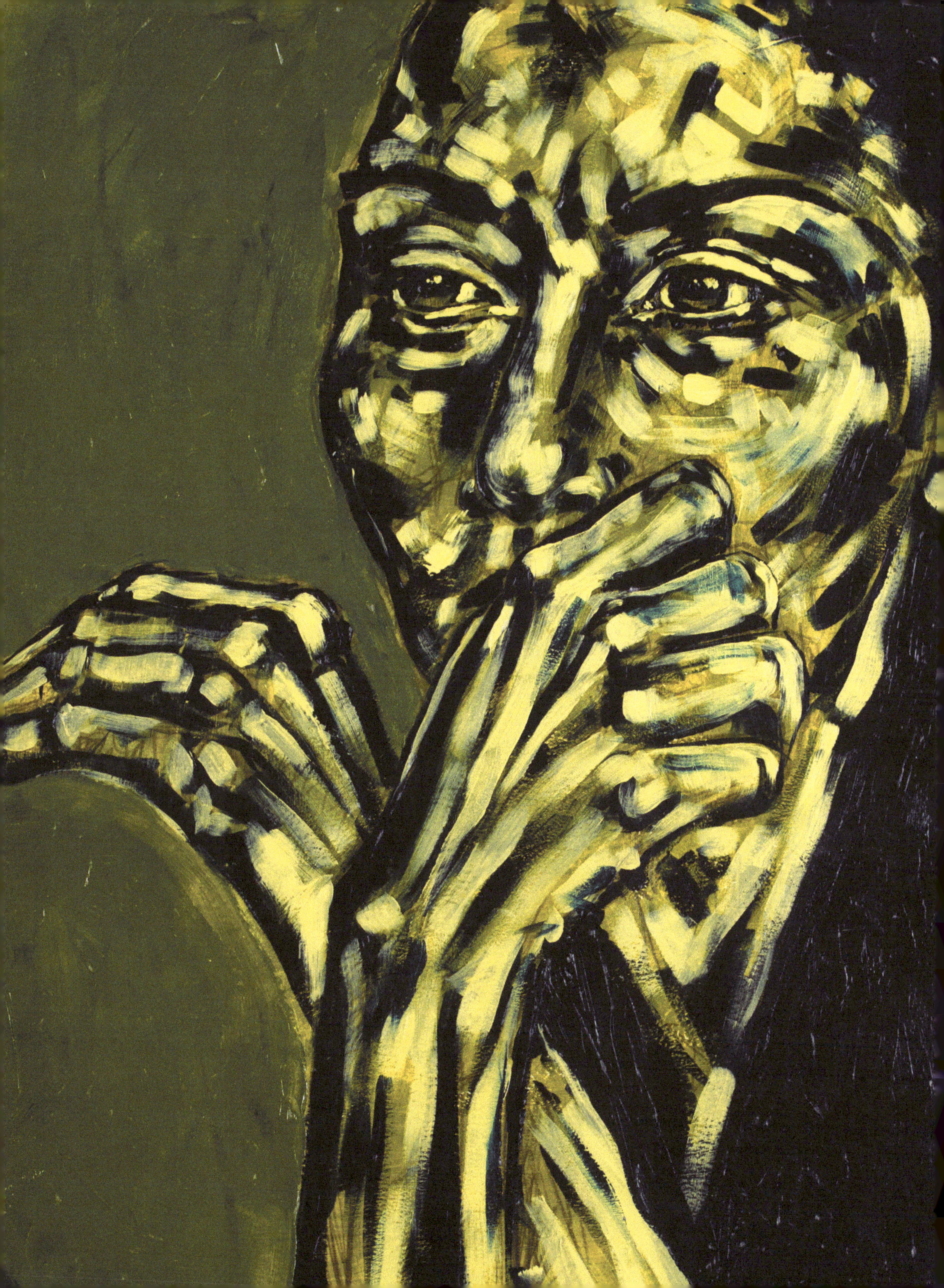

#17

DRASTIC

APRIL 13, 2020

Everything feels drastic today. . . things we are told to do, the things we choose to do. I feel drastic—my thoughts, emotions, decisions, choices—& it's not even in a negative way. . . it's just a lot. And even though I'm a person that LOVES change, this just feels drastic. How we deal with change is up to each person, each day. Today, for me, drastic feels right.

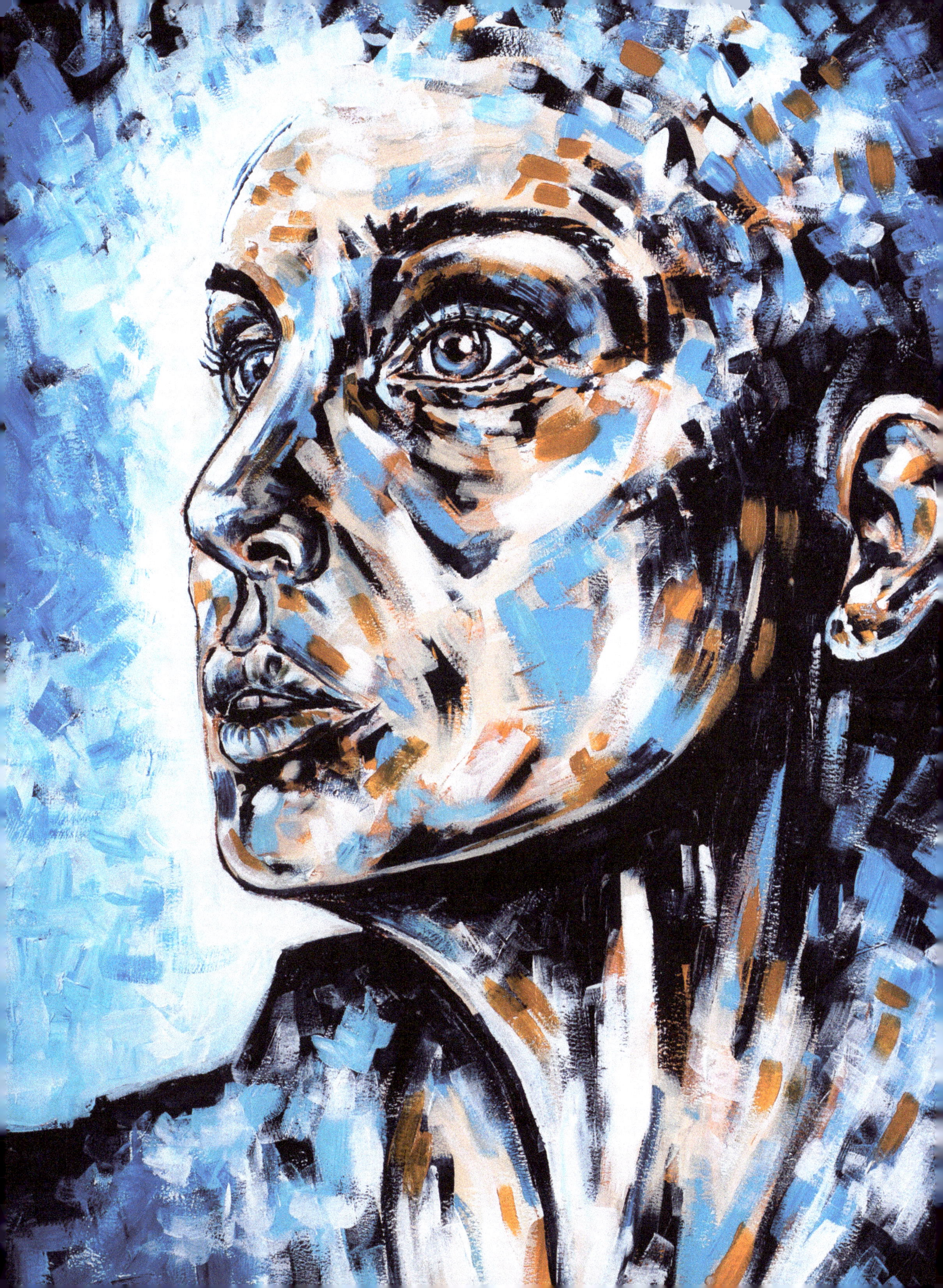

#18

DEFY

APRIL 14, 2020

I suppose I have some residual frustration built up right now, LOL. I think that we really are all working at "defying the odds" as they say & will come out on the other side sooner rather than later, but all this being good is making me want to be defiant. But I won't. I'll keep using my art to vent emotion & I know we all will defy these odds—this odd time—together.

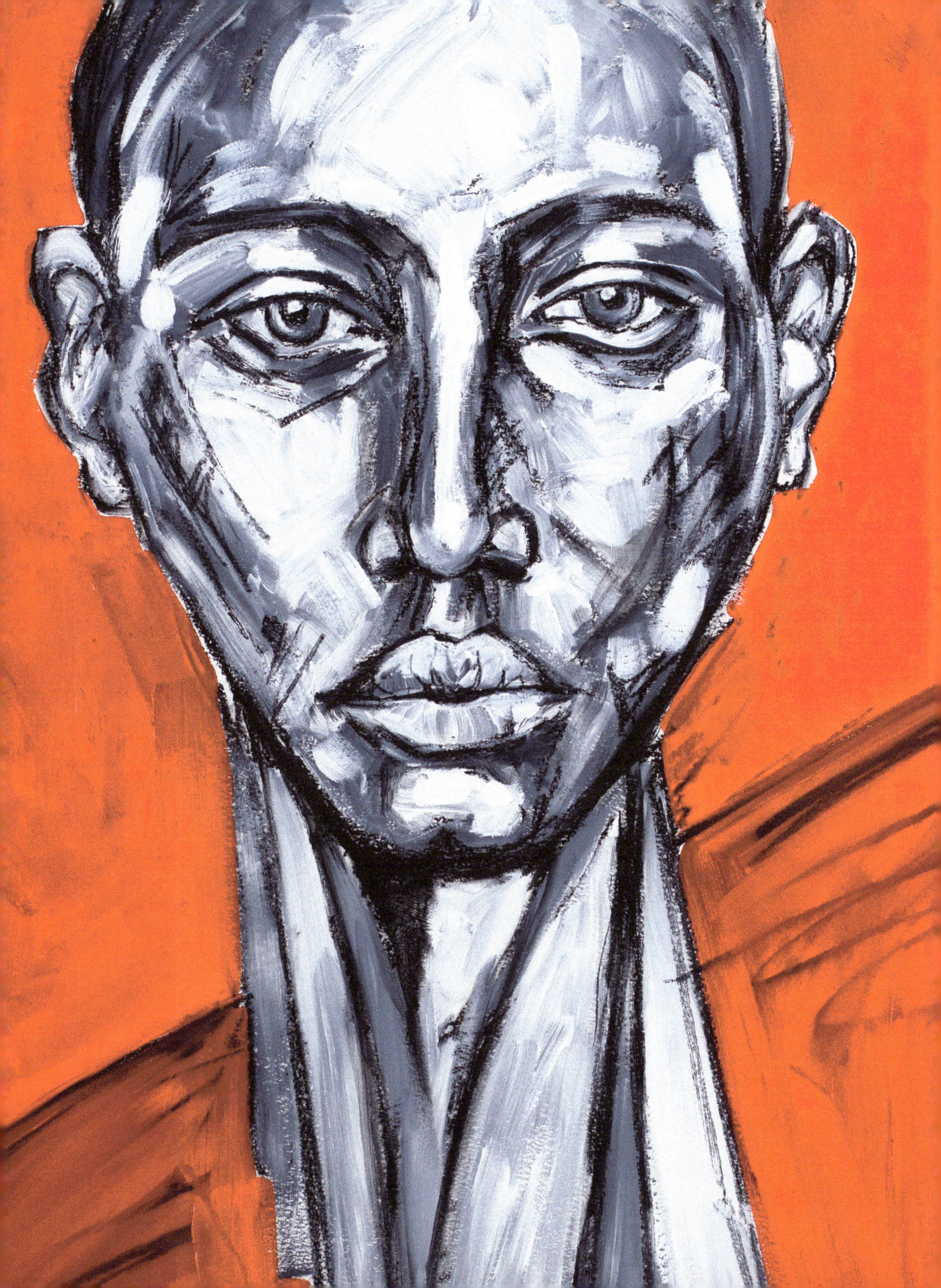

#19

OVERLOAD

APRIL 15, 2020

There's so much information coming at us every day & it changes—a lot. And then social media is bombarded with COVID articles & memes & theories. And then there's the conversations with your friends & family. And then this, & then that, & then there's more. My thoughts & opinions seem to change daily too. We must choose what we let into our minds. . . I think I'll press pause for a bit.

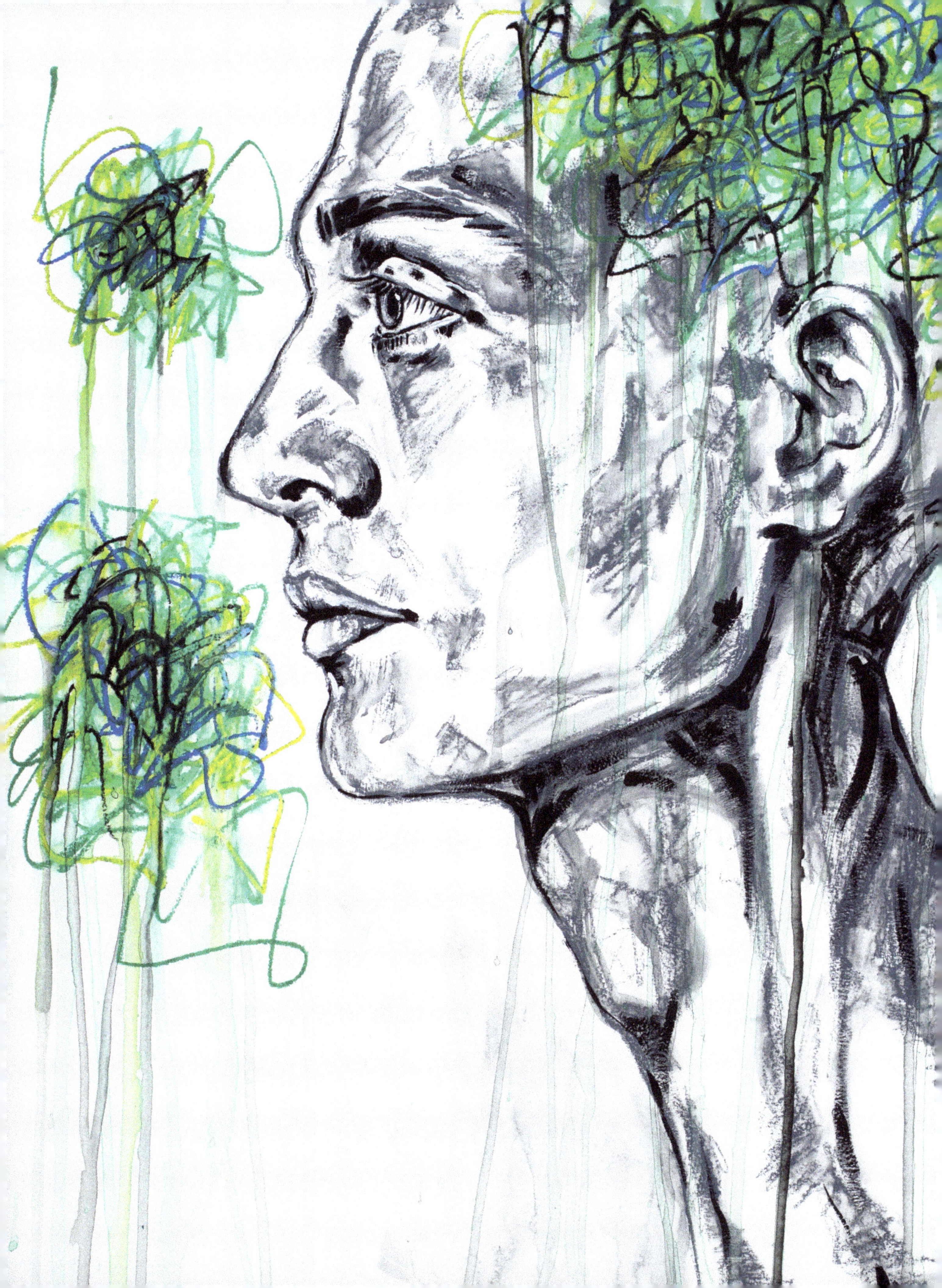

#20
PRESSURE
APRIL 16, 2020

Today I did not feel like doing my painting. I just did not care if I was productive or if I accomplished anything. . . I just felt like skipping it. I think we're all feeling that pressure though—all this "free" time—better get things done!! But I showed up & did it anyways. It was a quick one, but I still got it done—& this too will be part of my journey—the day I didn't want to create but did anyways. What are you doing today, in spite of how you feel?

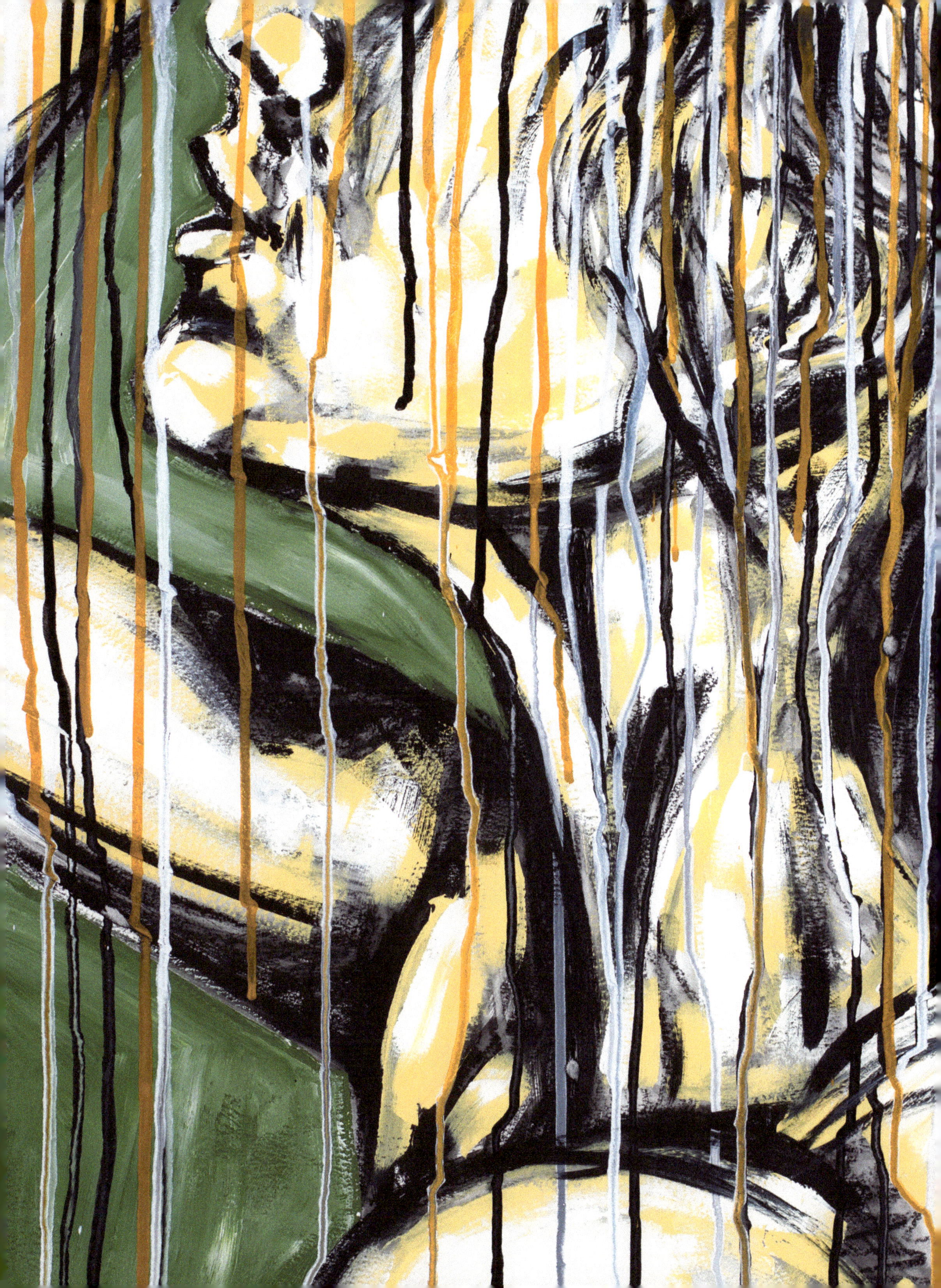

#21

DISTANT

APRIL 17, 2020

Thinking about before—then & now—does the past feel more distant, or maybe I just do? We're all told to "social distance" from each other, but does this play into how we feel in general? I think so. . . or maybe it's just today. It's not a bad thing, it just is. . . distant is a normalcy that just is right now. But you don't have to be distant in heart, & my heart is on my sleeve, pushing the distant away.

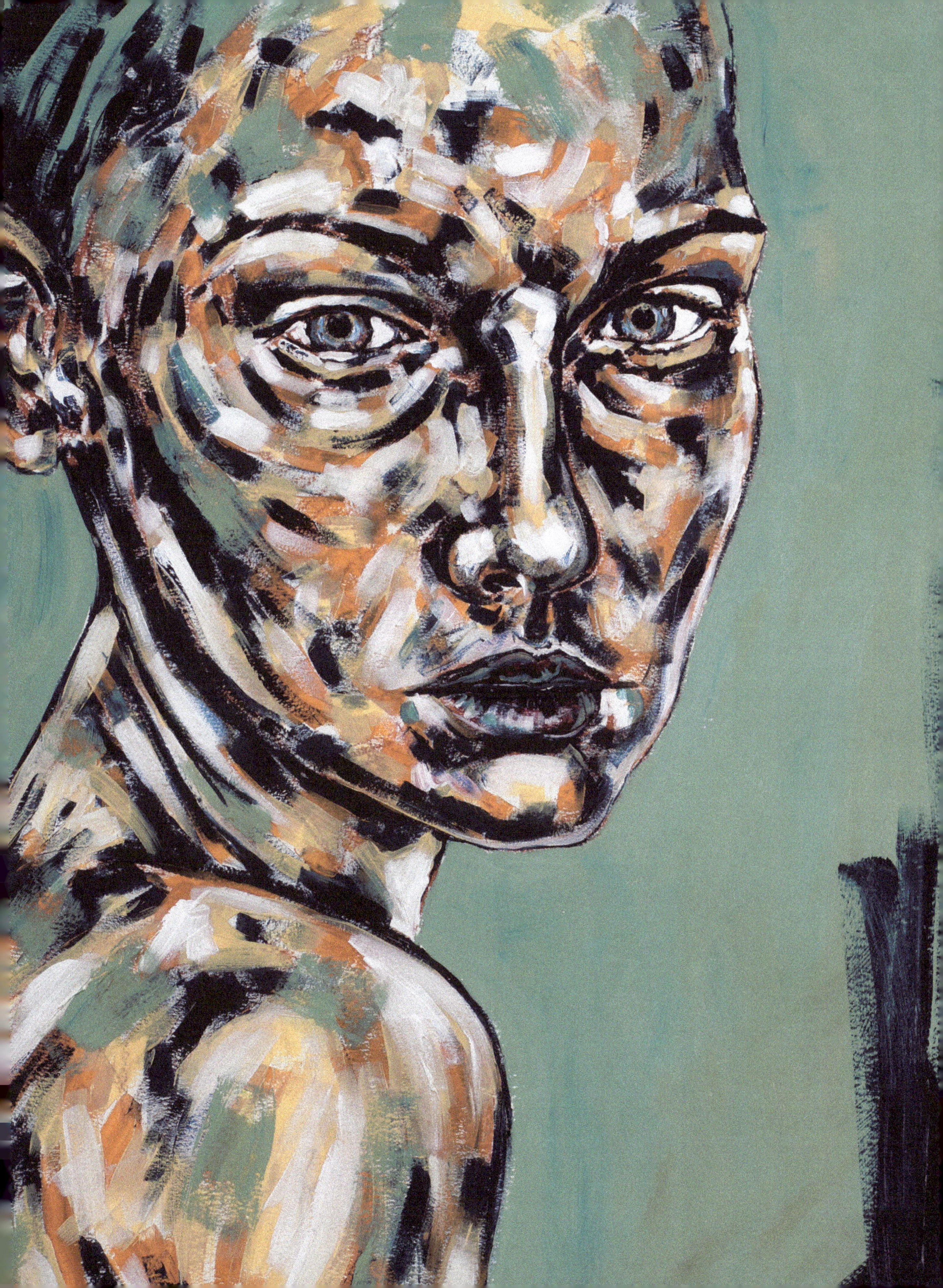

#22

BREAK

APRIL 18, 2020

Break the silence, break a leg, heartbreak, break the ice, break the law, breaking bad, to break, to be broken—it's all somewhere to start from. All of it makes you stronger & teaches how much you are actually capable of. Your breaking point might be exactly where you need to be & where you need to start from. When all hell breaks loose, this is when your greatest strength will come.

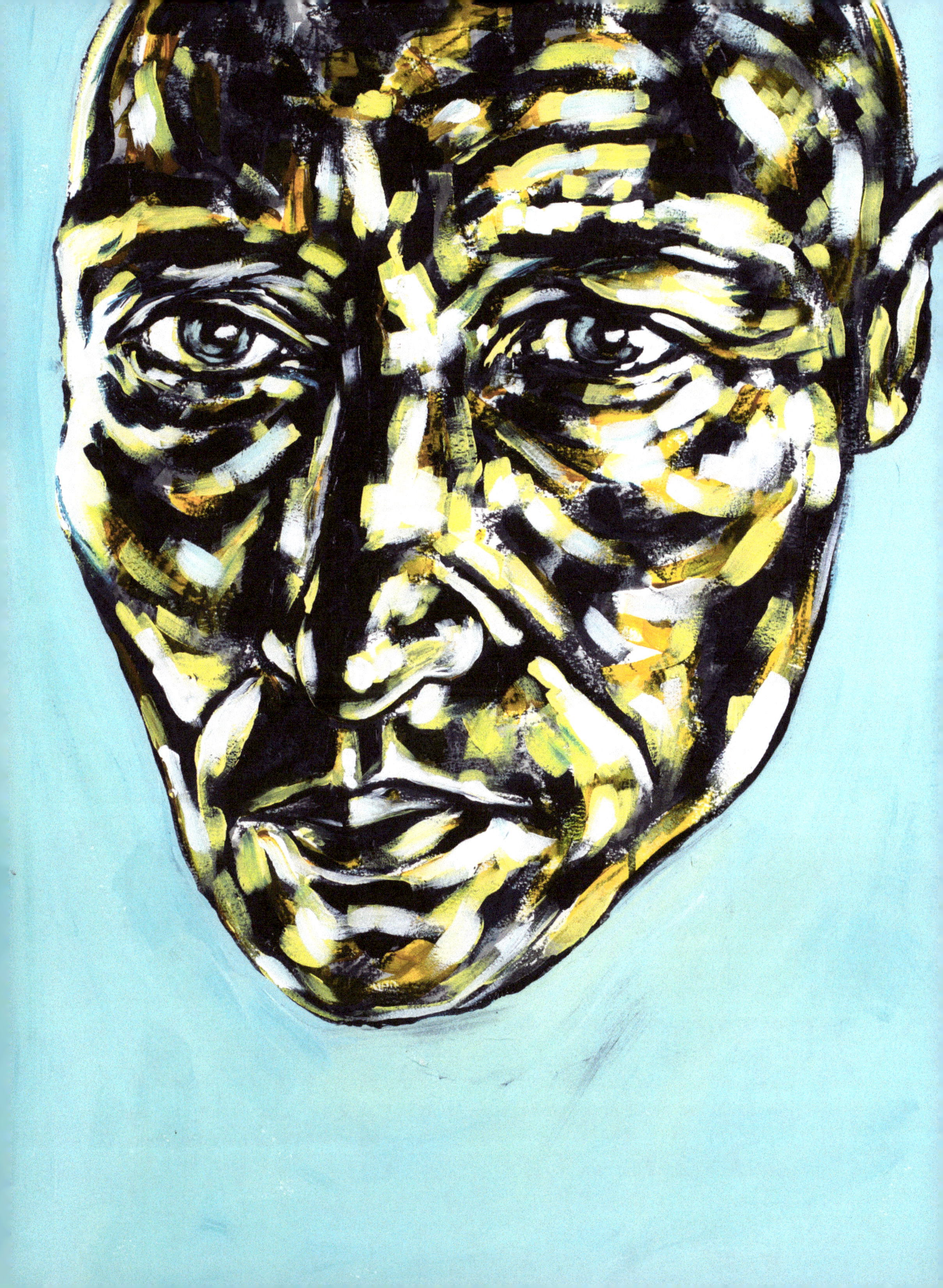

#23

NEXT

APRIL 19, 2020

As the days go by, some slower, some faster, I'm curious as to what the next chapter will bring. . . for us all but then, more selfishly, for myself. What's MY next chapter? Everything will change. No one knows for certain how things will be, or what our "next" will look like & we all will have some responsibility in that. What do you want your next to look like? The choices you make, even today, will contribute to your next. Pondering my next will be part of my now.

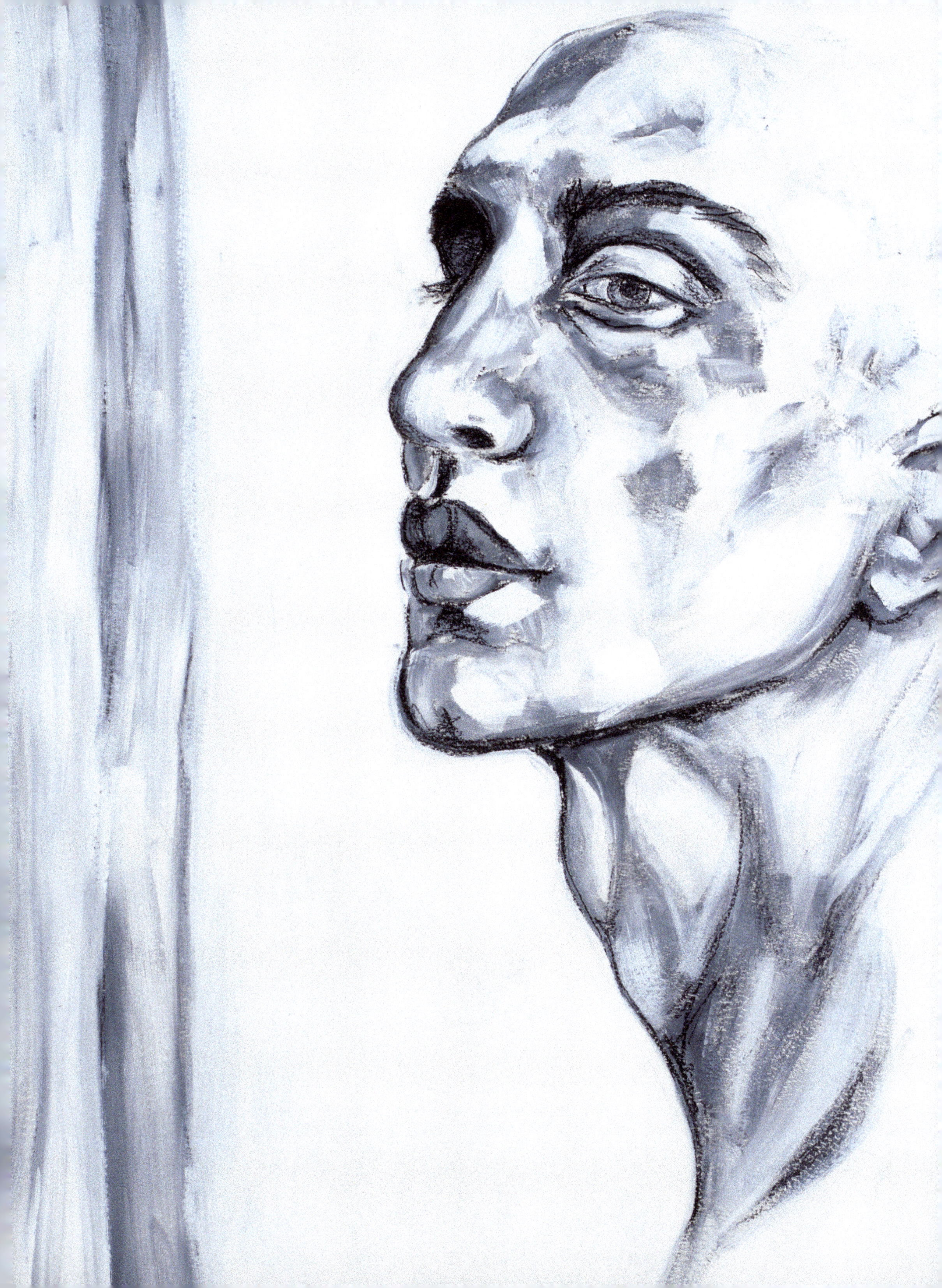

#24
STRENGTH
APRIL 20, 2020

You know that inner strength you have, the part of you that allows you to breathe through things & still remain standing (if not physically, then in your heart)? That's the strength I'm focusing on today—the strength where my confidence comes from in spite of conditions trying to convince me otherwise. We all have this strength. It's what will keep us being our true selves amidst adversity. Our true selves are amazing.

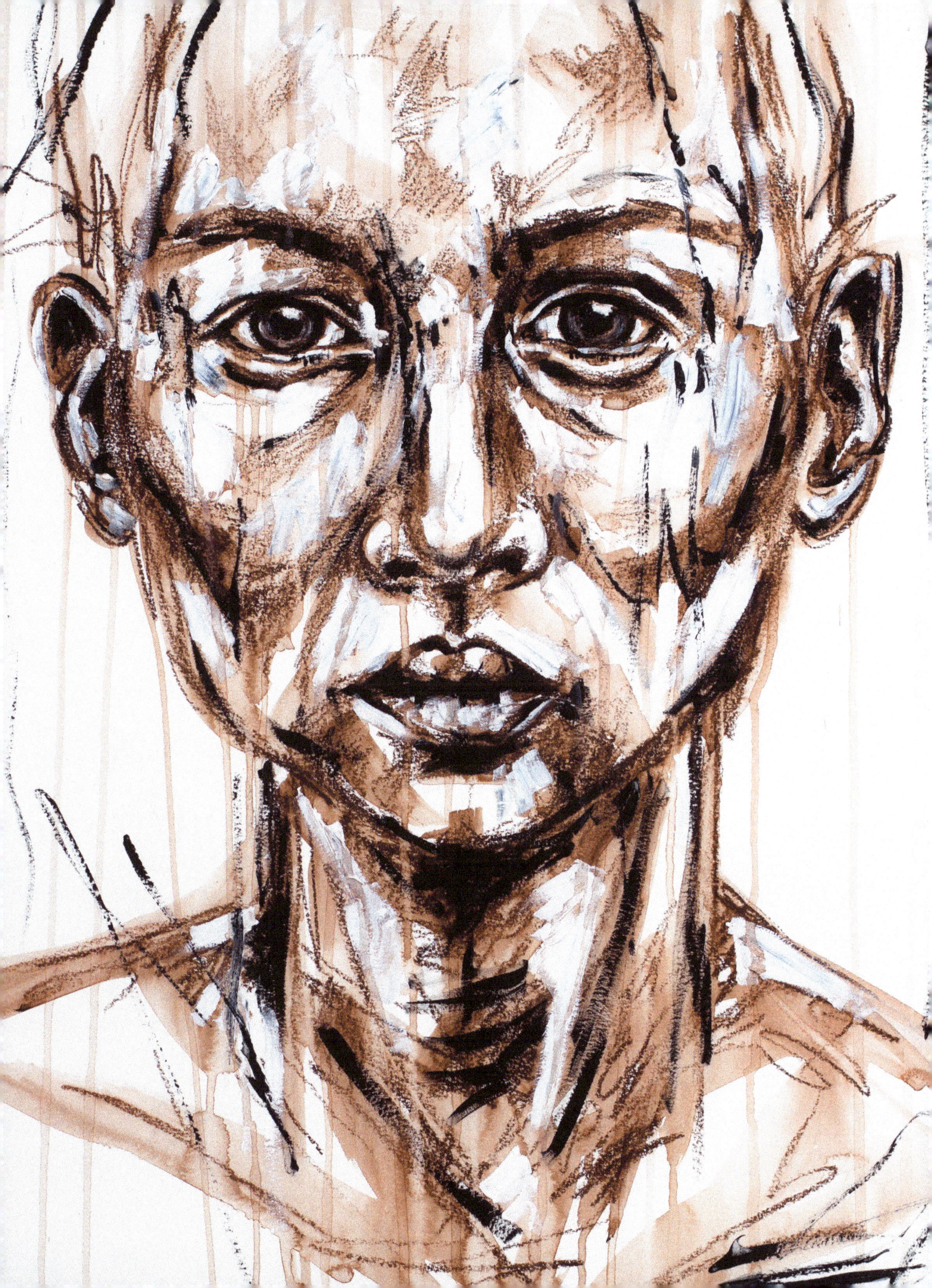

#25

HONEST

APRIL 21, 2020

Is it difficult to be honest with yourself during unprecedented times? I'm finding it curious—the things I've realized about myself, spending more time than ever before alone—I'm finally, truly listening to myself—nothing to pull me away from me. I'm having honest conversations with heart & mind. Spending years of giving myself excuses, justifying actions, convincing myself (rather easily over time) that I was already being the honest me, when in actuality, I hadn't given myself the time to figure out who that was. . . until now.

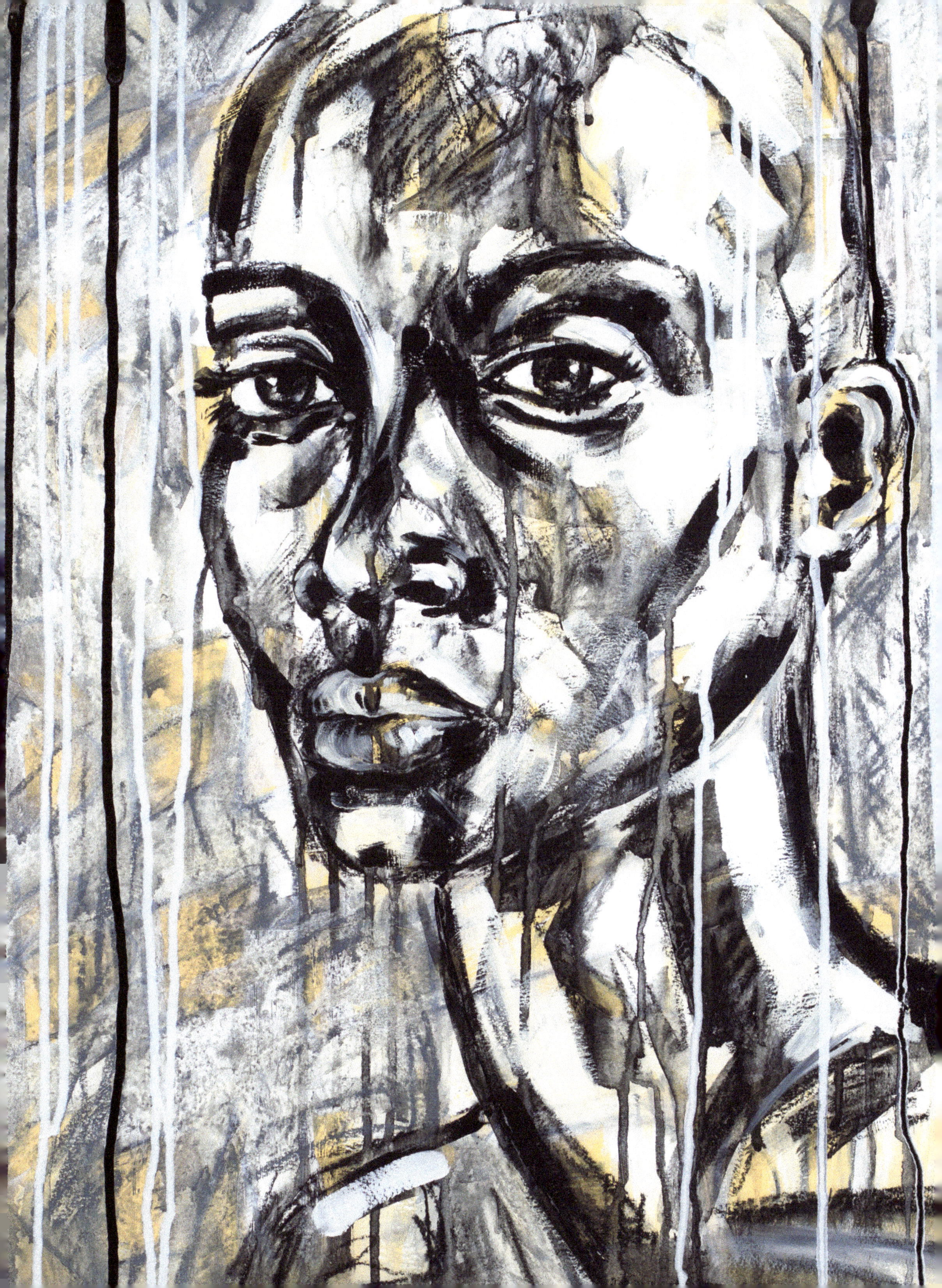

#26

QUESTION

APRIL 22, 2020

So many questions, so few (if any) answers. Even though we know we have to wait this out, it doesn't stop us from asking a million questions a day—it certainly doesn't stop me. Most are about the current situation, but more & more are about formulating my own personal journey & what I want for myself now & after. Questioning is about thinking & brainstorming, but also knowing that I have to be okay with letting go of the need for instant answers. All answers will come at the right time.

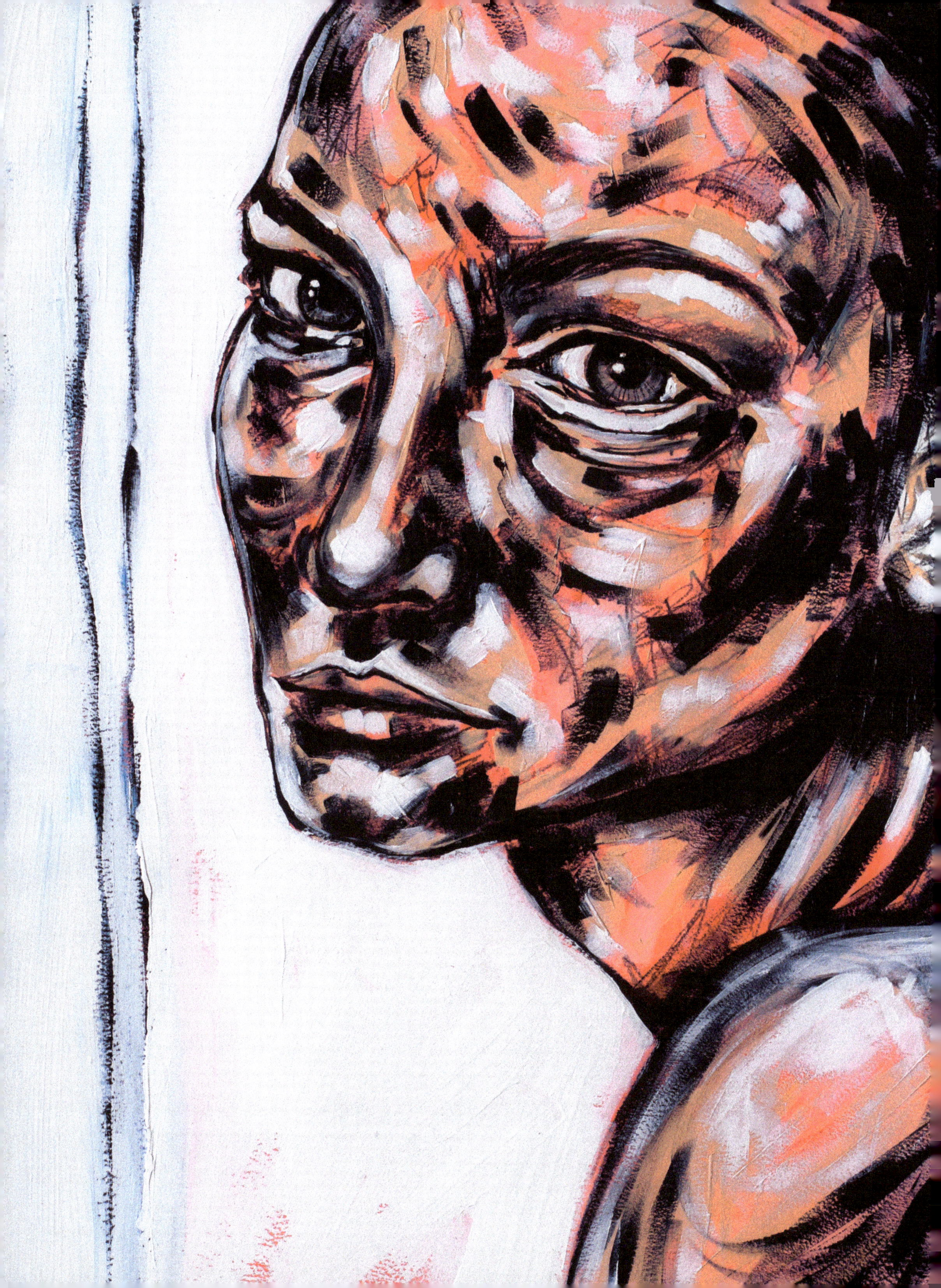

#27

RESTLESS

APRIL 23, 2020

I would bet we're all feeling a little restless & stir crazy like a caged animal. Trying to be at peace with the current situation is difficult & being aware & present & really living in the moment is challenging, but so worth the practice. I might be on the verge of climbing the walls, but I am going to (TRY) & use this as my moment to just be. Be aware. Be present. And maybe, also to run around the block, LOL.

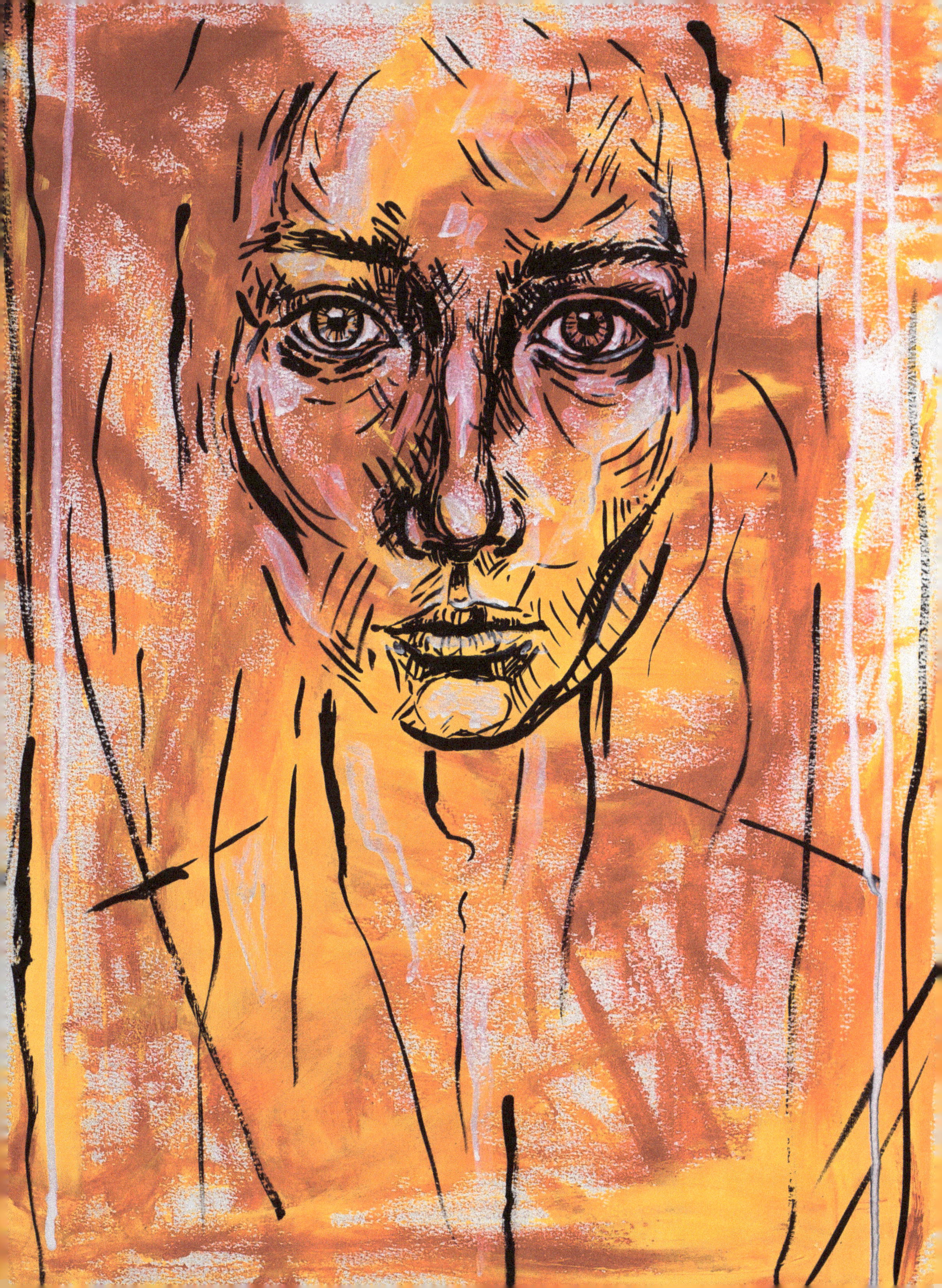

#28
NOSTALGIA
APRIL 24, 2020

I went for a hike this morning with a friend (yes, we were social distancing, LOL) but it felt so normal. I almost forgot what was going on in the world, then when I did remember, I started reminiscing about things. Isn't it funny how one little thing that feels so normal, can take you away for a moment, but then you snap back as soon as you say, "Ooh, where should we go for lunch?" I think it's okay to be nostalgic, but also be reminded that there are magical little opportunities every day, like my morning hike. We must do the things that take us away, even for a short time, just to feel happy.

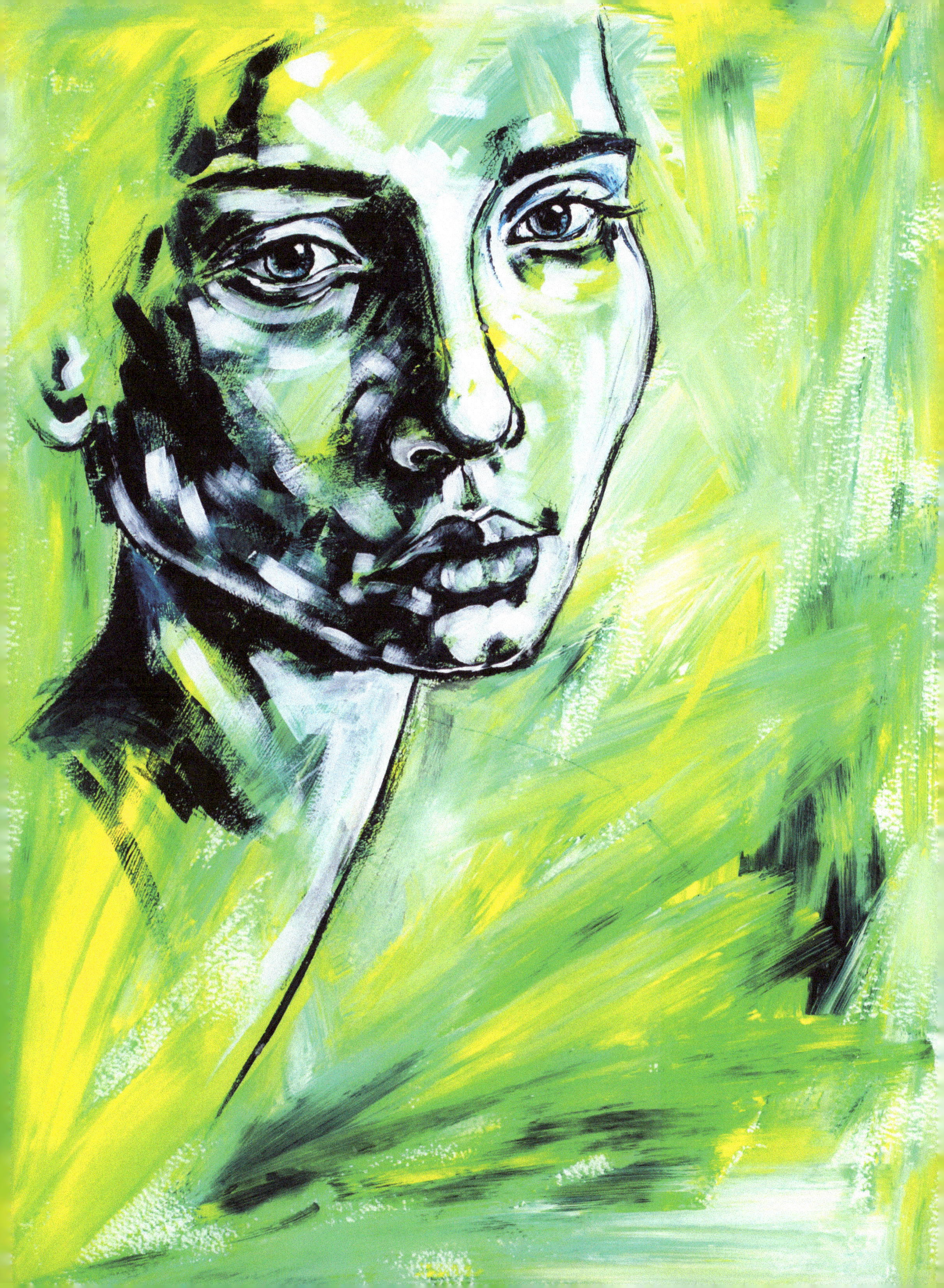

#29

COMPASSION

APRIL 25, 2020

I've always been a bit (or a bunch) of an empath—trusting, emotional, rooting for the underdog—& right now we're all kind of underdogs, so to speak. We all desperately need to have, & need to give, compassion. We may all be in this together, but it's a completely different journey for every single one of us, regardless what you believe is happening. I've been so touched & encouraged by people's responses to this series, & for me, that's my compassion received. I urge us all to spread some of our own compassion & know we all have the ability to uplift one another.

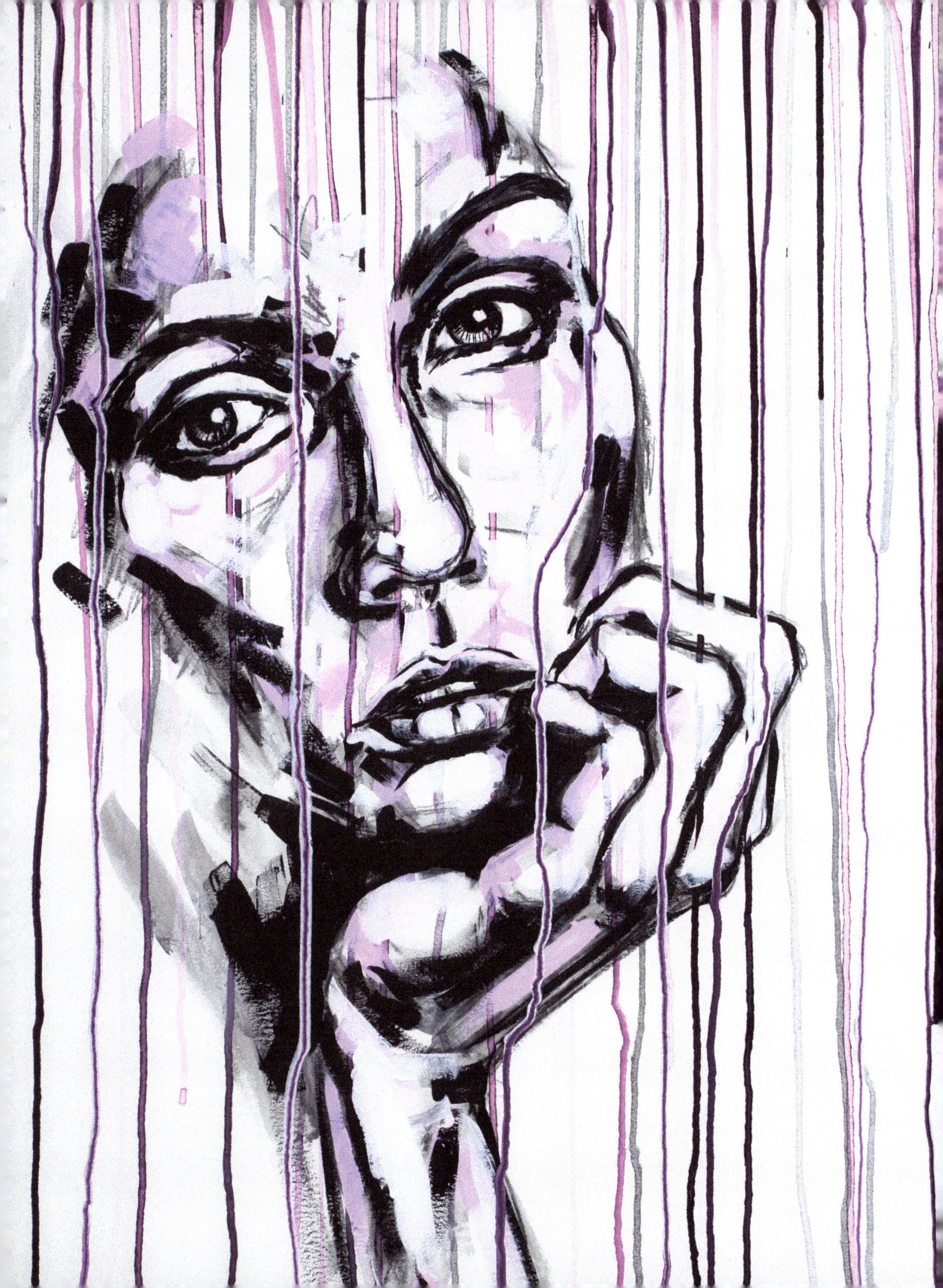

#30

BORED

APRIL 26, 2020

The days are all kind of running together. I have my own routine of exercise & art, writing & reading, but then what? Maybe the motivation runs out after that, or maybe I'm just plain bored! Today I was so bored that I put acrylic paint on my face to apply it to this canvas (all the orange in the background was put on with the right side of my face). Getting it off my face was another story! (LOL!) I guess we just have to think up weird little things to fill our days with right now, & maybe some of them will turn into interesting stories we can tell later, when we're finally out with friends.

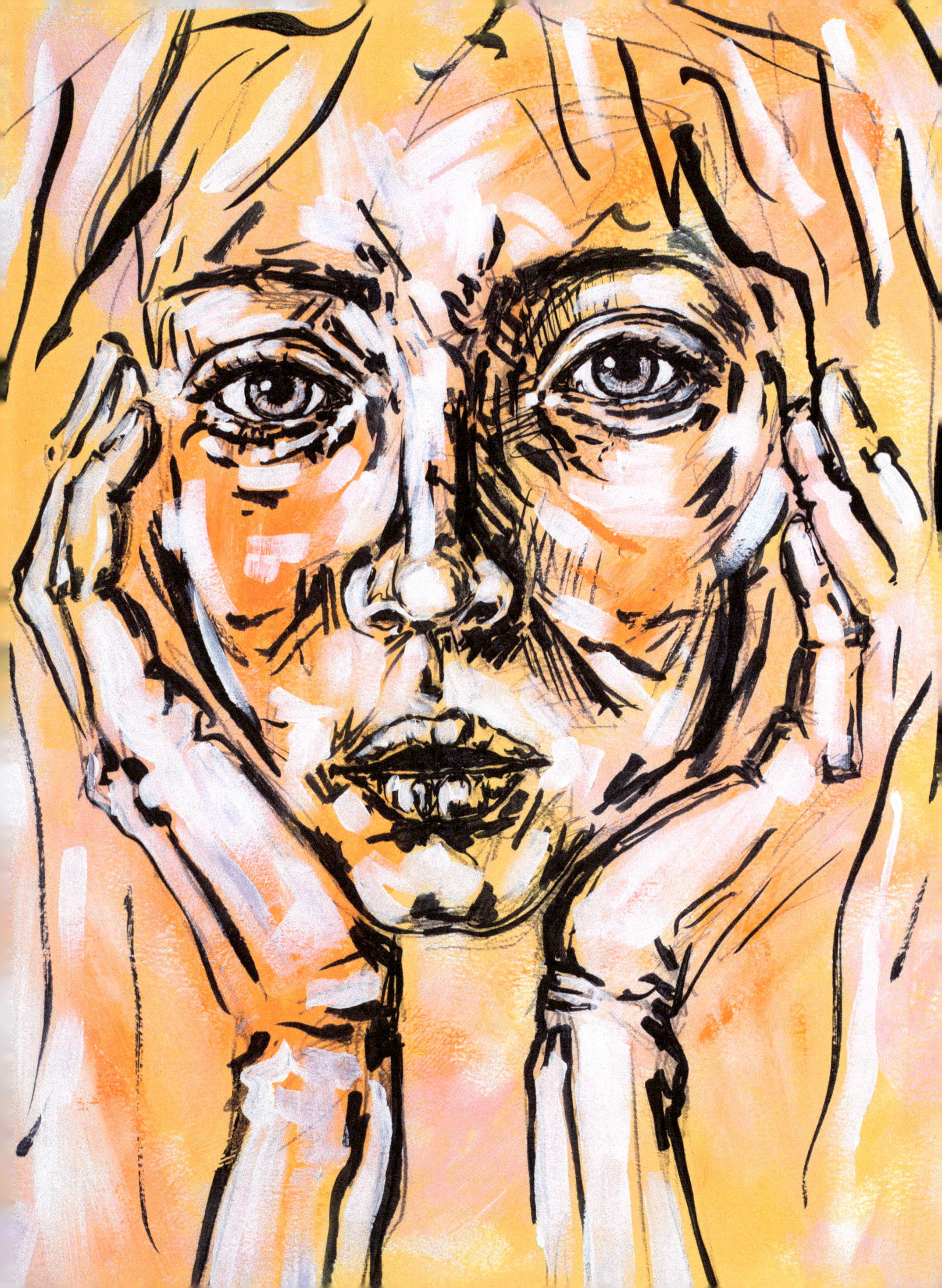

#31

SPIRIT

APRIL 27, 2020

We may feel tired, grumpy, anxious or bored, or we might feel grateful, at peace, creative or happy, but whatever we feel on any given day, there is one thing that can't be taken away from us: our spirit. We can always have comfort & strength in knowing that we are still our unique selves, constantly changing, but forever our own. We are proving every day just how strong our spirit truly is & how much the world needs each & every one of us.

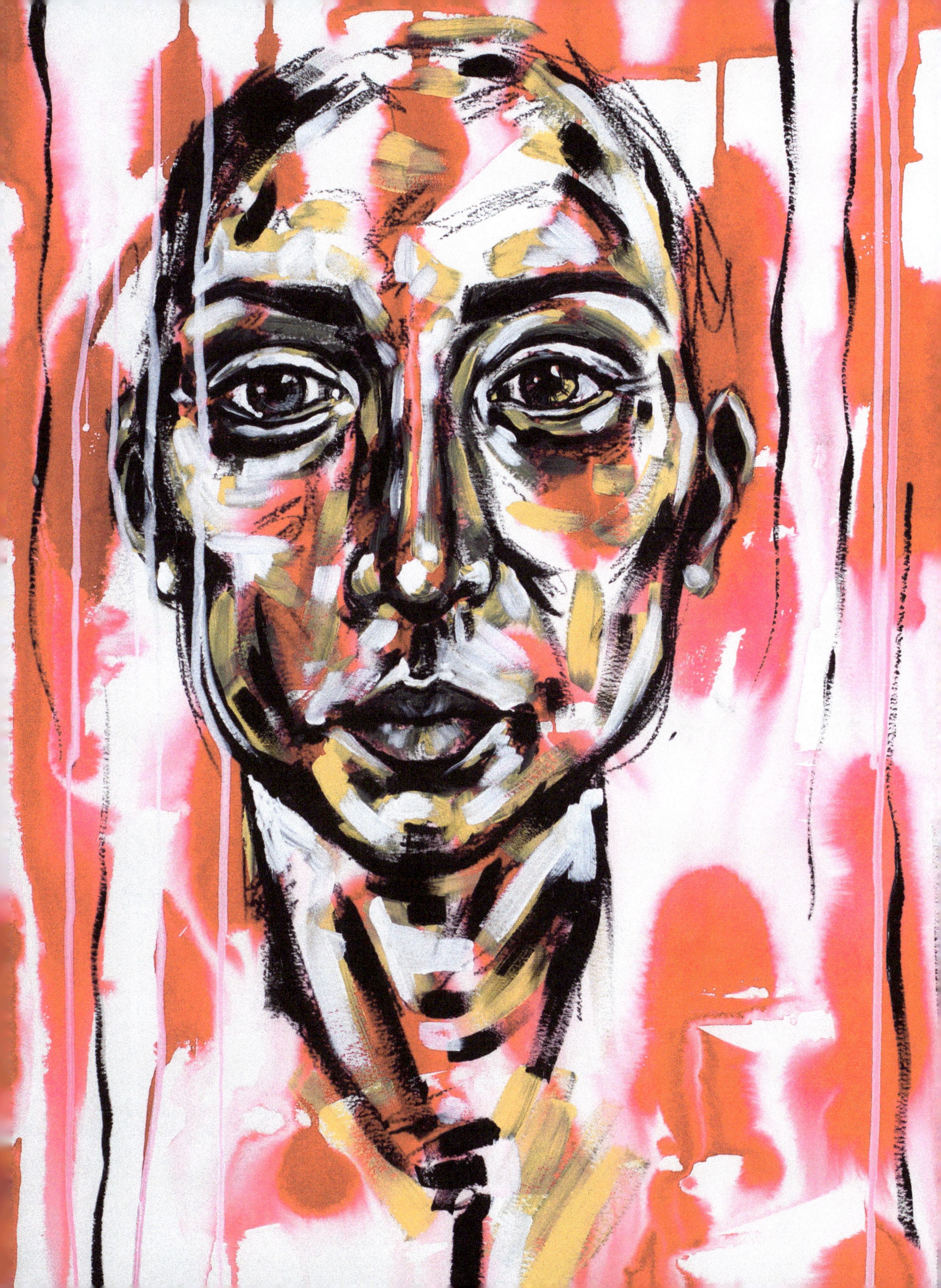

#32

AUTHENTIC

APRIL 28, 2020

I think that now, having been at home without any social time for about 35 days, I'm figuring out who my "self"' is. I'm not saying I wasn't "me" before, but when you're in solitude, authentic thoughts, dreams, actions come out. What do I really want after all this? Who do I really want to be? What would a true AUTHENTIC life look like? I'm doing things that make me feel the most like ME right now. The trick will be continuing these things when we get to other side of this, with the clarity & conviction to be our authentic selves.

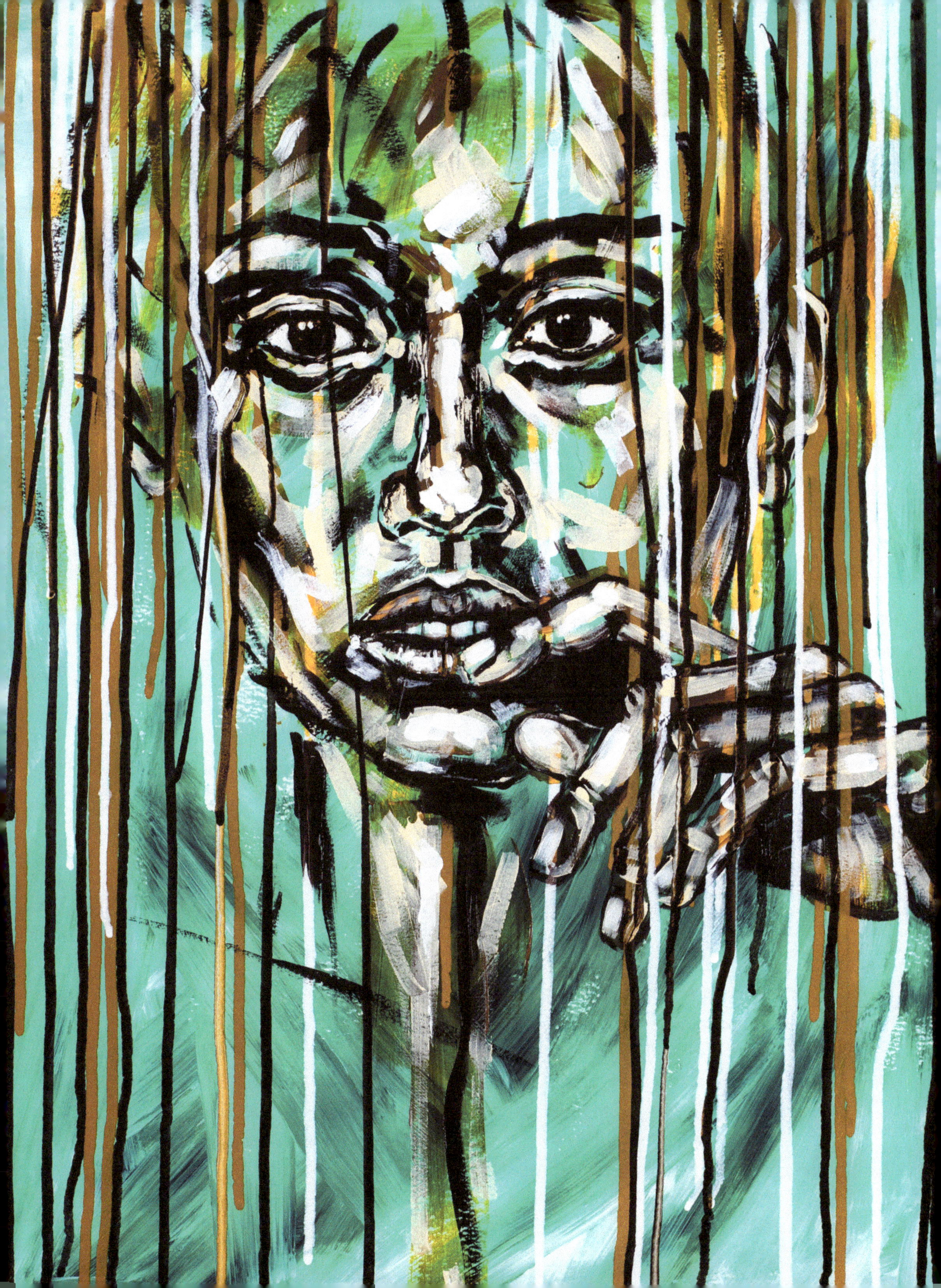

#33

MOVE FORWARD

APRIL 29, 2020

I think, to really be ready when restrictions start to ease up, & to really be ready to move forward, we're going to have to lessen the opinions we listen to, lessen the "facts" we take as truths & lessen the chatter we're a part of. To really move forward, we have to see with our heart & shut all the noise off. As our normal has changed, & will continuously be changing, how do we want to move forward? I want to have less words & more action, less mindless & more mindful. I want to really MOVE FORWARD & there's no time like the present to start these steps forward.

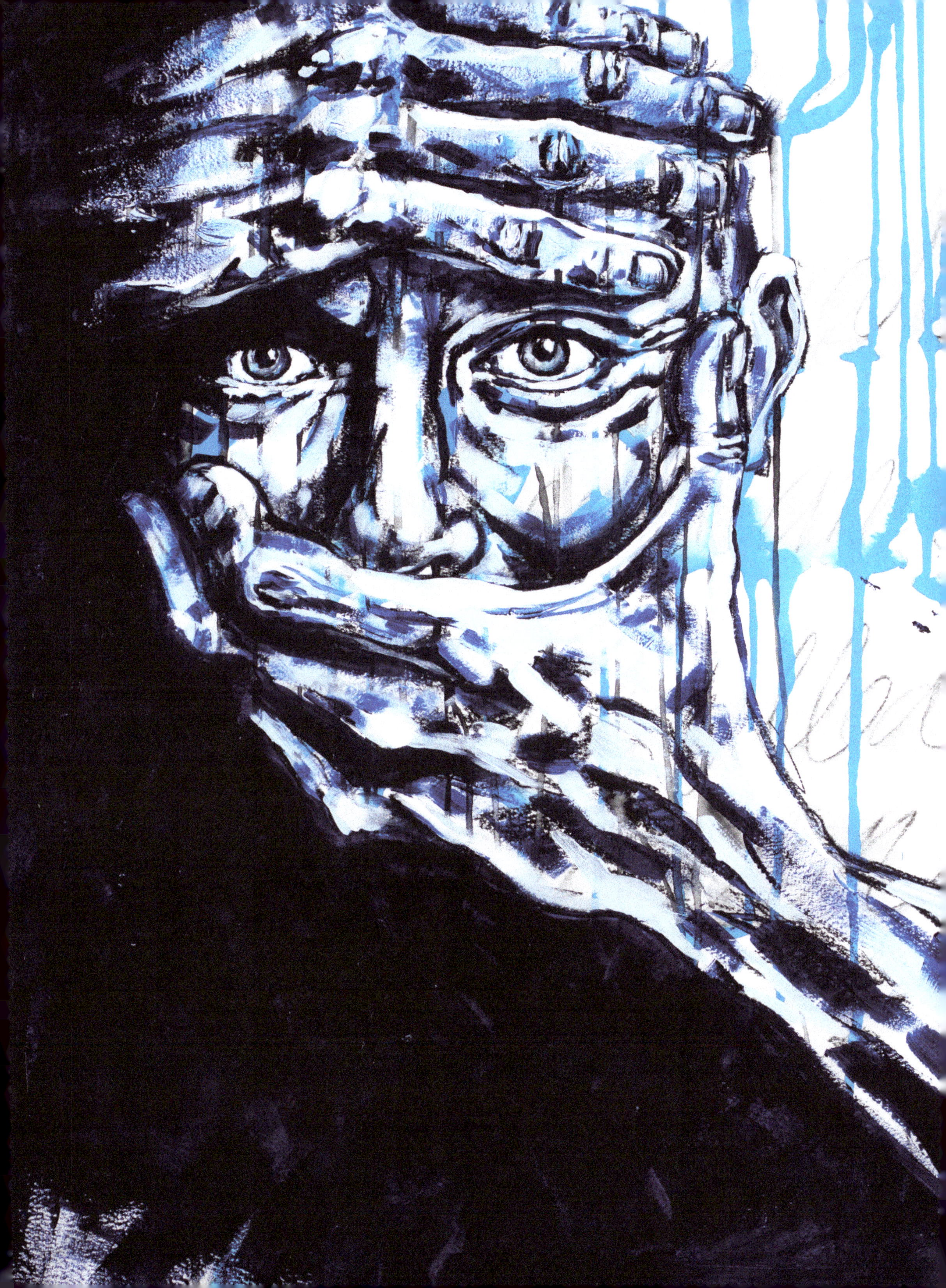

#34

WORRY

APRIL 30, 2020

Honestly, I'm not a huge worrier. I try to roll with the punches, but these past few weeks I've had my share of worried moments, but now that there are murmurings of things starting to reopen (which is obviously great) I've been having more worried moments than before. I'm not exactly sure why, but I think it's due to finally returning to "reality." Only it won't be the reality I remember, & there's no way any of us can know what to expect. I guess when we were told to stay home, that's all we could do, but now that we might be able to go back to work & socialize with friends, what will that look like? I'm a person that loves change, but change that comes with a bunch of rules? (Not so much, LOL.) I guess we can only wait & see & continue to roll with the punches.

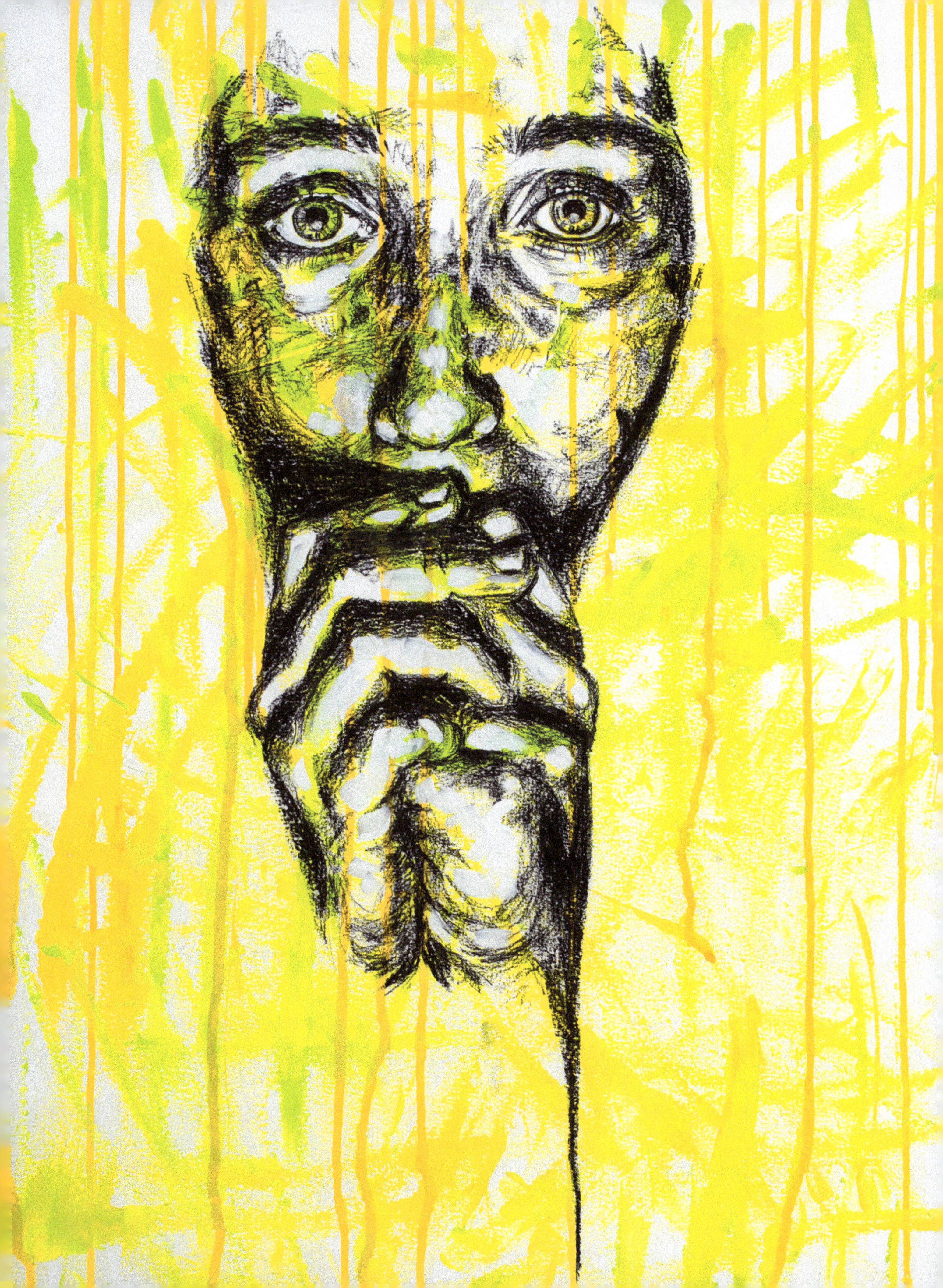

#35

SPORADIC

MAY 1, 2020

Yup, I'm all over the place lately—definition: scattered or isolated—pretty much sums me up (& maybe some of you?). Happy, freaked, helpless, peaceful, content. . . both excited & scared of what's to come. . . & again, there's no right or wrong feeling or opinion about what's happening. We just have to be aware, remember our priorities & practice self-care. The next chapter is around the corner, so let's all just be kind. Amidst all the other crazy emotions we feel, let's just be kind.

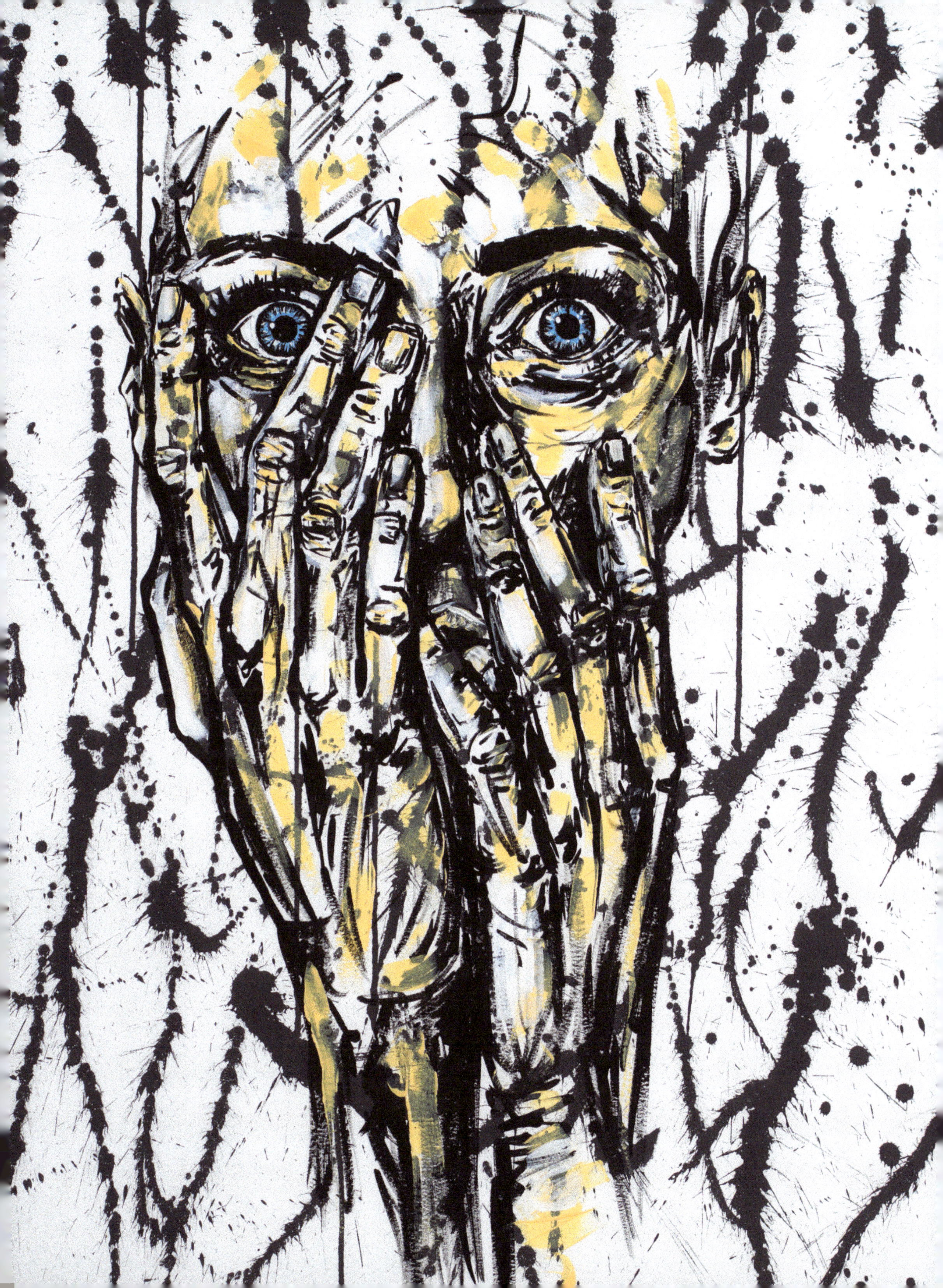

#36

FAITH

MAY 2, 2020

I was going to name this something cheeky like *the blind leading the blind*, which does ring true right now. But then I thought, what do you do when you can't see what's next, or what's in front of you? You step out in faith, trusting that you will land firmly. I think that we all have & need faith, whether it's in God (I know I've said my share of little prayers lately), humanity, the universe, your own strength, or in all of the above. We all need faith to trust in right now—to trust that without seeing what's next, we will prevail.

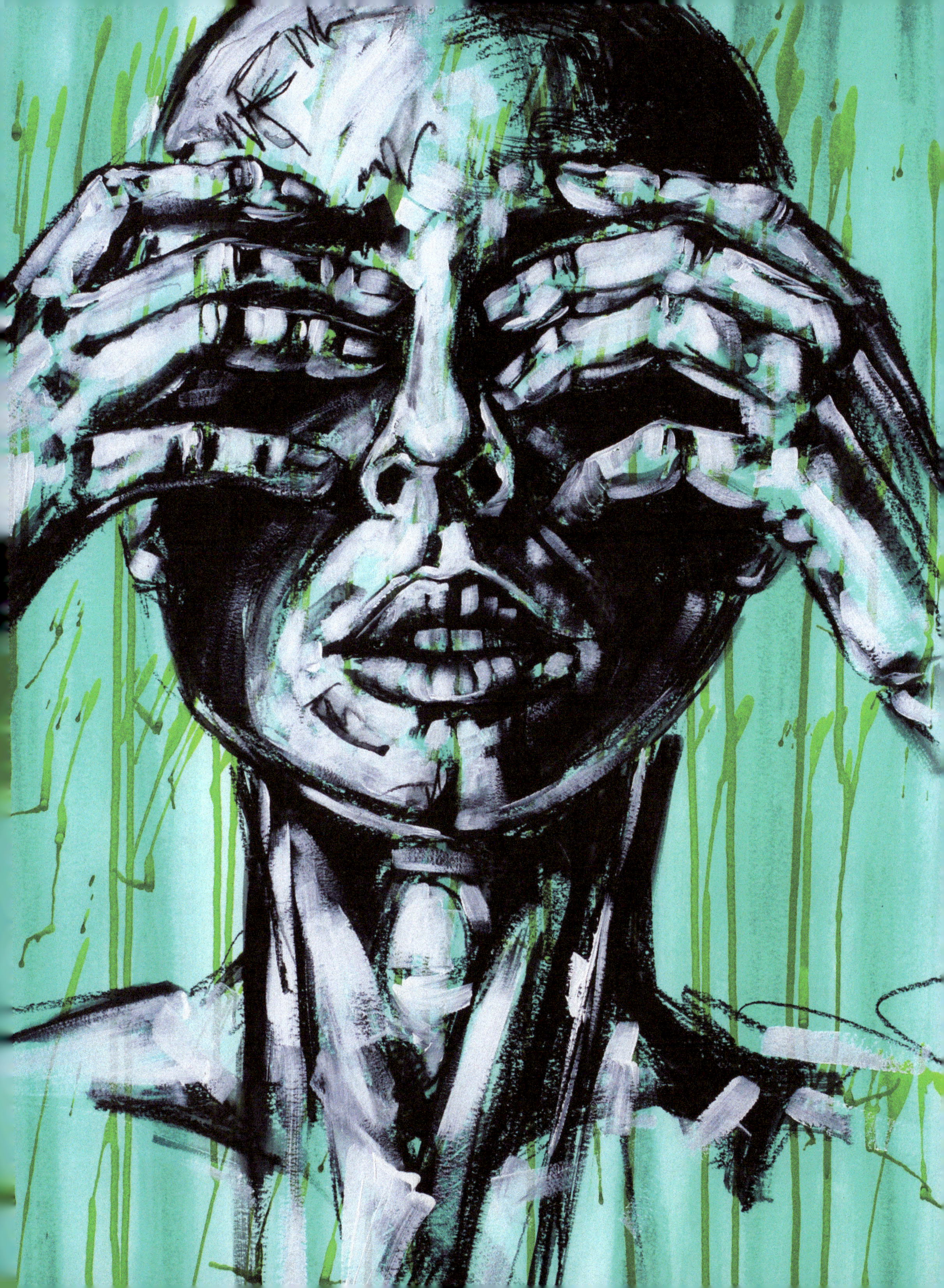

#37

DISINTEREST

MAY 3, 2020

As the shock value of this whole pandemic/isolation/lockdown time wears off. . . as the funny memes get repetitive. . . as the opinions get more controversial. . . I just find I'm getting more & more disinterested in all of it. Maybe it's just today's mood, but I'm kind of over it. It'll be what it'll be, & we'll all adjust to each new parameter, but the craziness of it all is fading. I guess that's in part due to our adaptability. We're just in the grey area of it all. There's no clear black & white in any of this, so let's all enjoy the day & all we have to be grateful for.

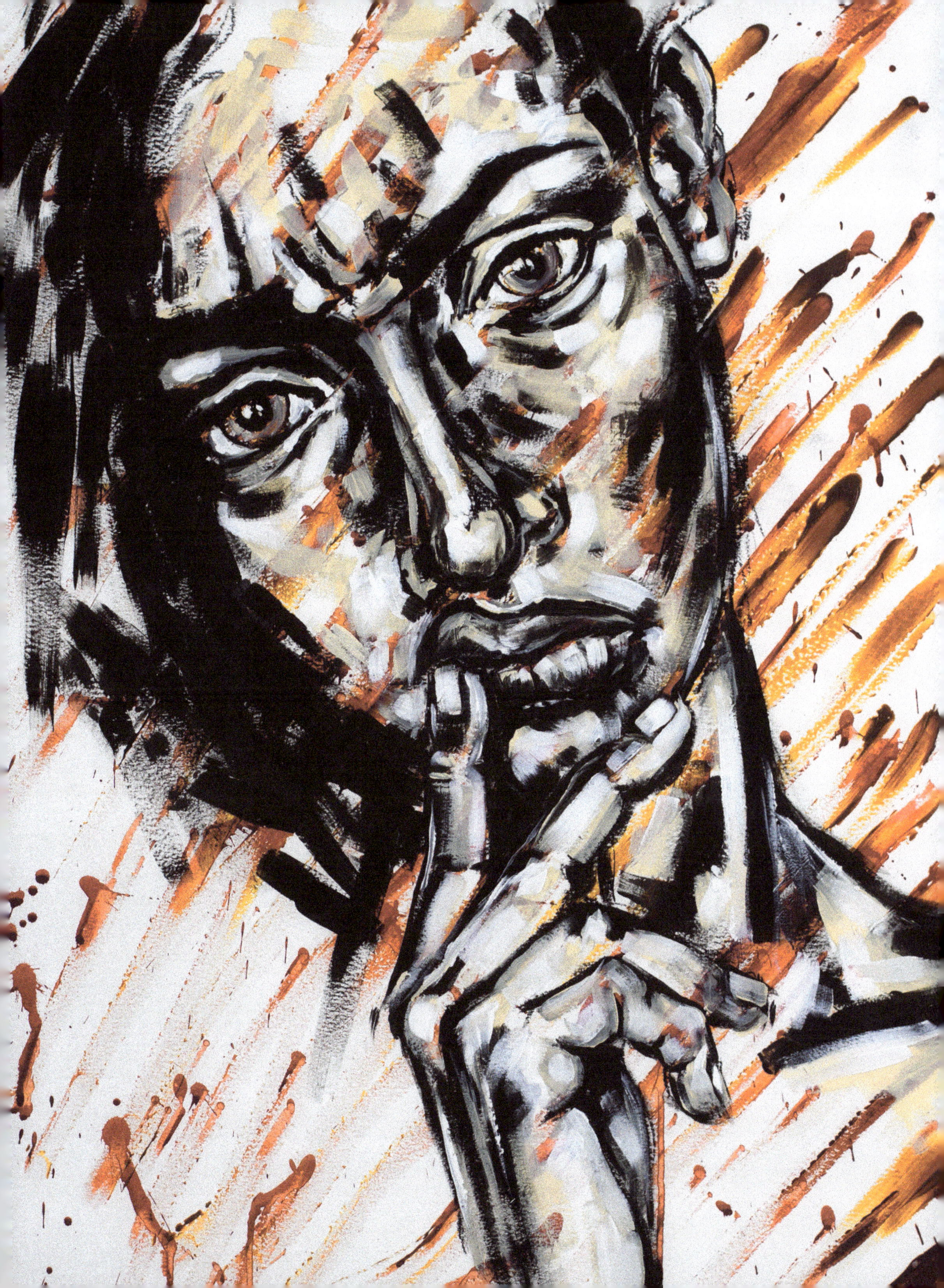

#38

MONOTONY

MAY 4, 2020

We've all heard the jokes about feeling like we are living out the Bill Murray classic *Groundhog Day* with every day blurring into the next with no definite end in sight. I don't even know if I mind it. I mean, really it's up to us, so choose your happy & work it into your daily routine. While it's easier than ever to fall into monotony right now, we can all get creative & change it up—cut your own hair, draw on the walls, naked kitchen-dance, prank call your friends—do what it takes to make your day fun!

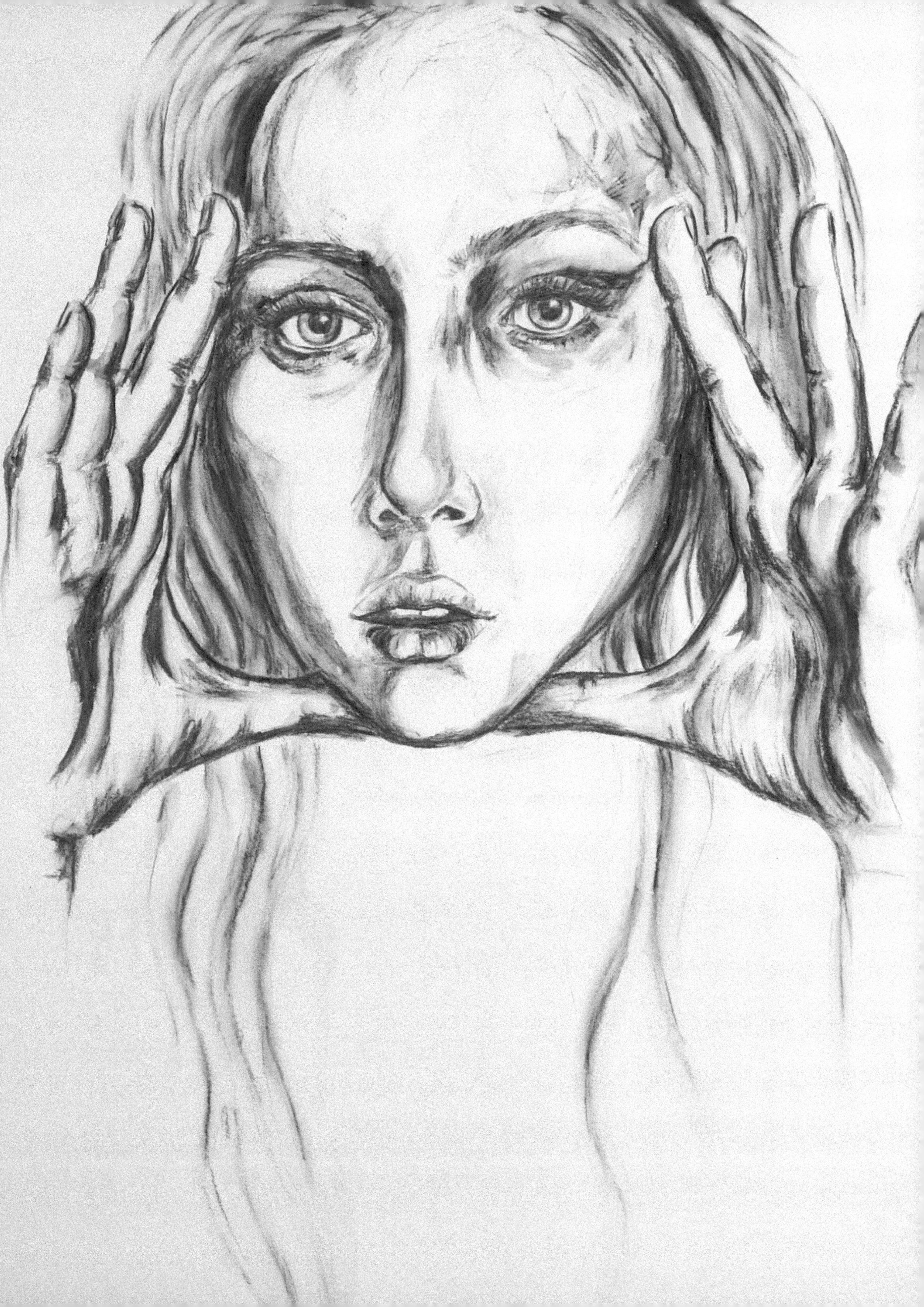

#39

NEVER

MAY 5, 2020

They say, "never say never," & honestly, they're right (whoever "they" are). I would never have thought any of this could or would ever happen, not in a million years. But that's how life is: what's around the next corner, no one knows. BUT they also say, "NEVER give up," & that's the 'never' to focus on. Fall down 7 times, get up 8.

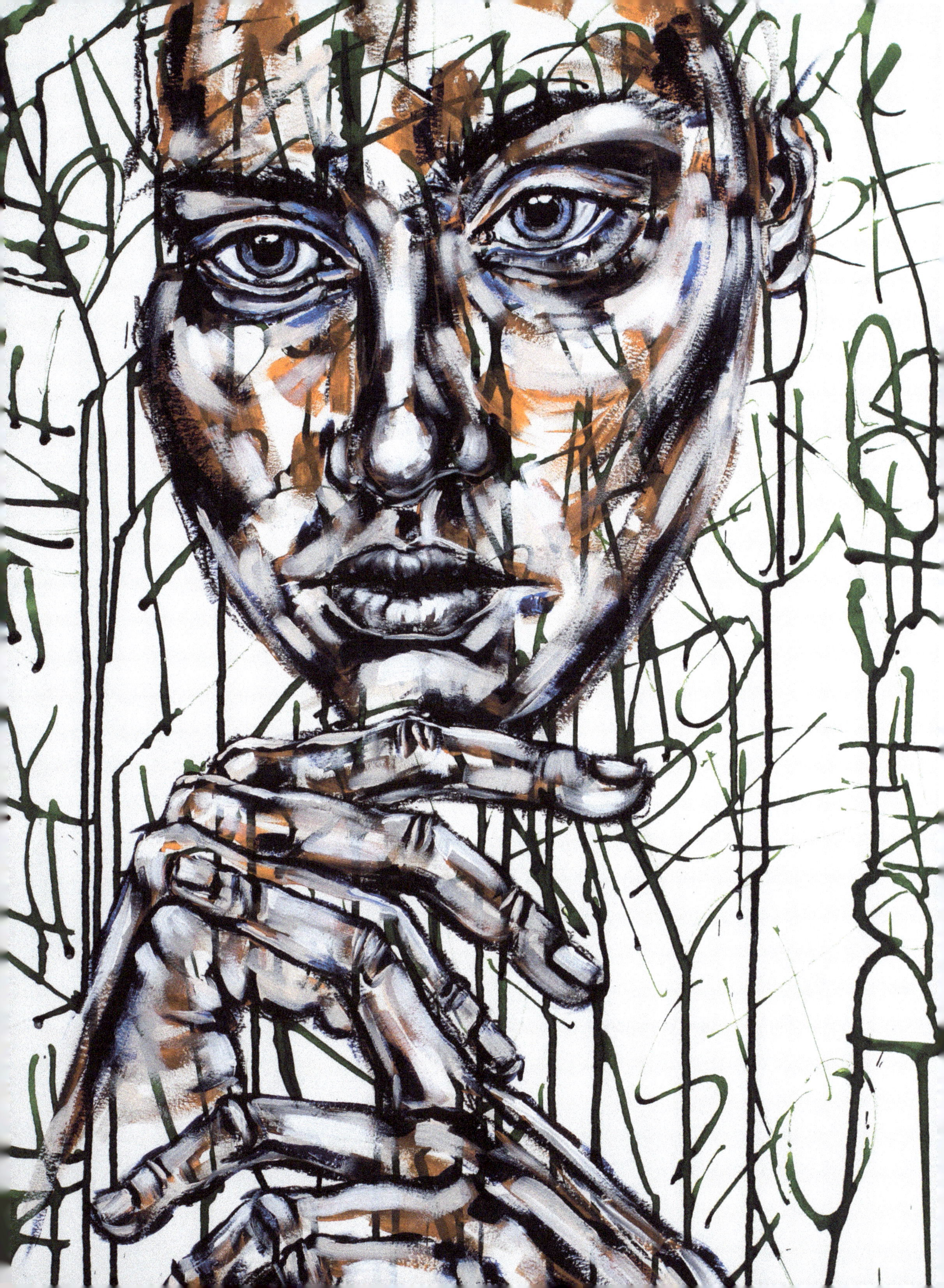

#40

BE HAPPY

MAY 6, 2020

Well, I woke up grumpy this morning—don't know why. . . just the day—& today's rain goes nicely with it. I'd also like to thank the people in the apartment above me for tearing apart their kitchen today. The constant hammering & sawing added to my grumpiness for sure. I'm usually a "choose happy" type of person, but you have to just accept what you're feeling too. Especially right now, if this pandemic & self-isolation time has taught me anything, it's to embrace ME. To embrace exactly who I am, right now. We are all enough. And we don't need to be happy every moment. Choose happy when you can & give me 20 minutes of no more hammering from above & I will too.

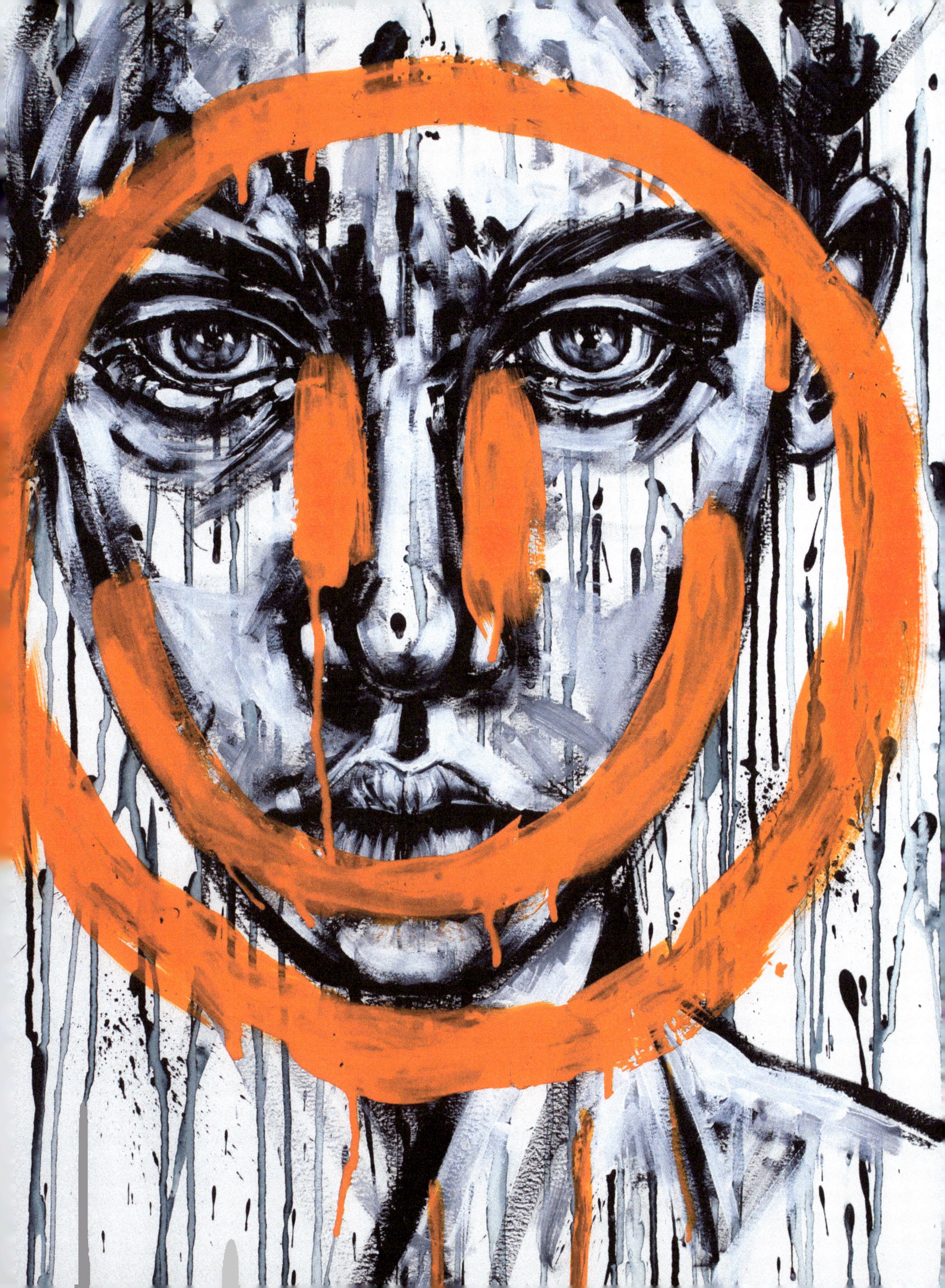

#41

ILLUSION

MAY 7, 2020

There are so many unknowns at this point. WHEN we can re-enter society & WHAT it will even look like at that point & HOW will it evolve? It kind of seems like an illusion—a suggestion of reality—a mirage that we can't quite get to. An illusion is a thing that is, or is likely to be, wrongly perceived or interpreted by the senses. What is your perceived notion of what we are going back to? Whatever it is, let's all put effort into making it a better, kinder & simpler place than before.

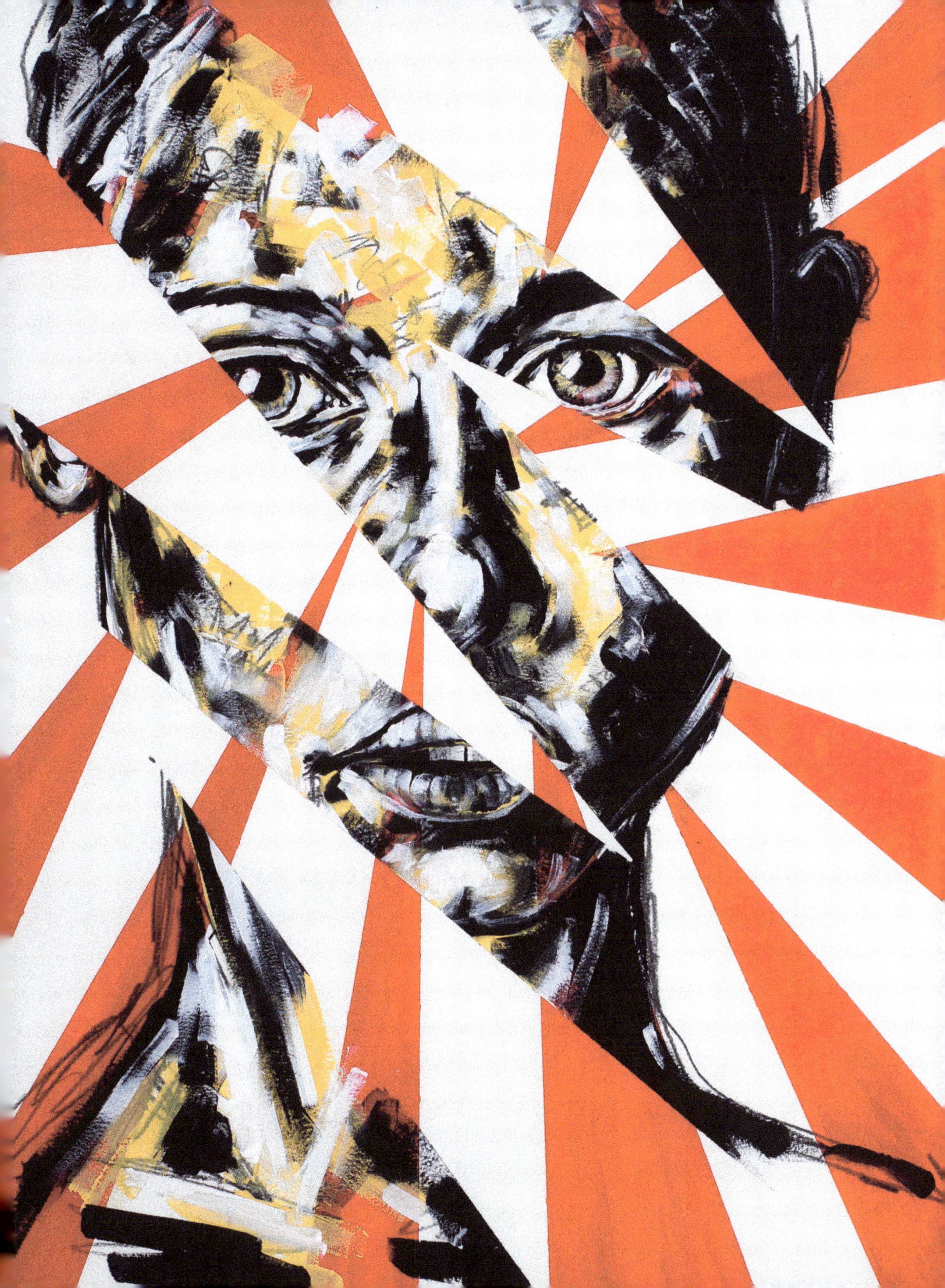

#42

DISTORTED

MAY 8, 2020

Do we all have a distorted memory of how amazing our reality was before all this craziness happened? Are we blowing it up in our minds because it's been a couple of months since we've lived it? Do we have a distorted vision of the reality we'll be going back to? The list of what isn't distorted might be shorter nowadays. I think as long as we move forward with better intentions, a little distortion now & again couldn't hurt.

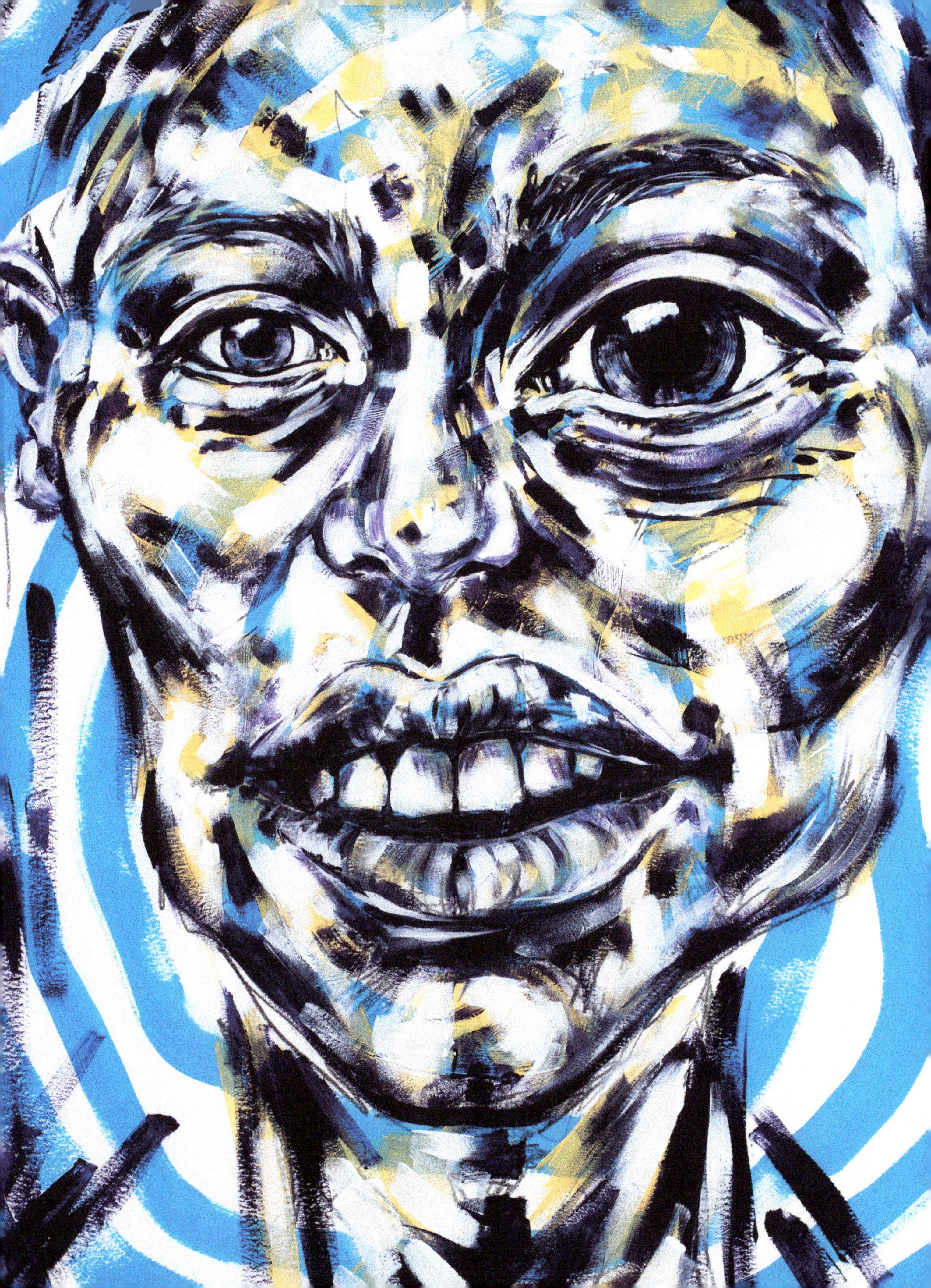

#43

HUMAN

MAY 9, 2020

I was doing some errands this morning & I have to say that small gestures go a long way. I mean, none of us really knows how to act out there. It all feels awkward—jumping out of people's way, cautiously moving around—but when you see a smile or share a little laugh with someone, it makes all the difference. We're all human, we just want kindness. Let's all put extra effort into giving more of these little moments to each other. I mean, underneath it all, we're all the same.

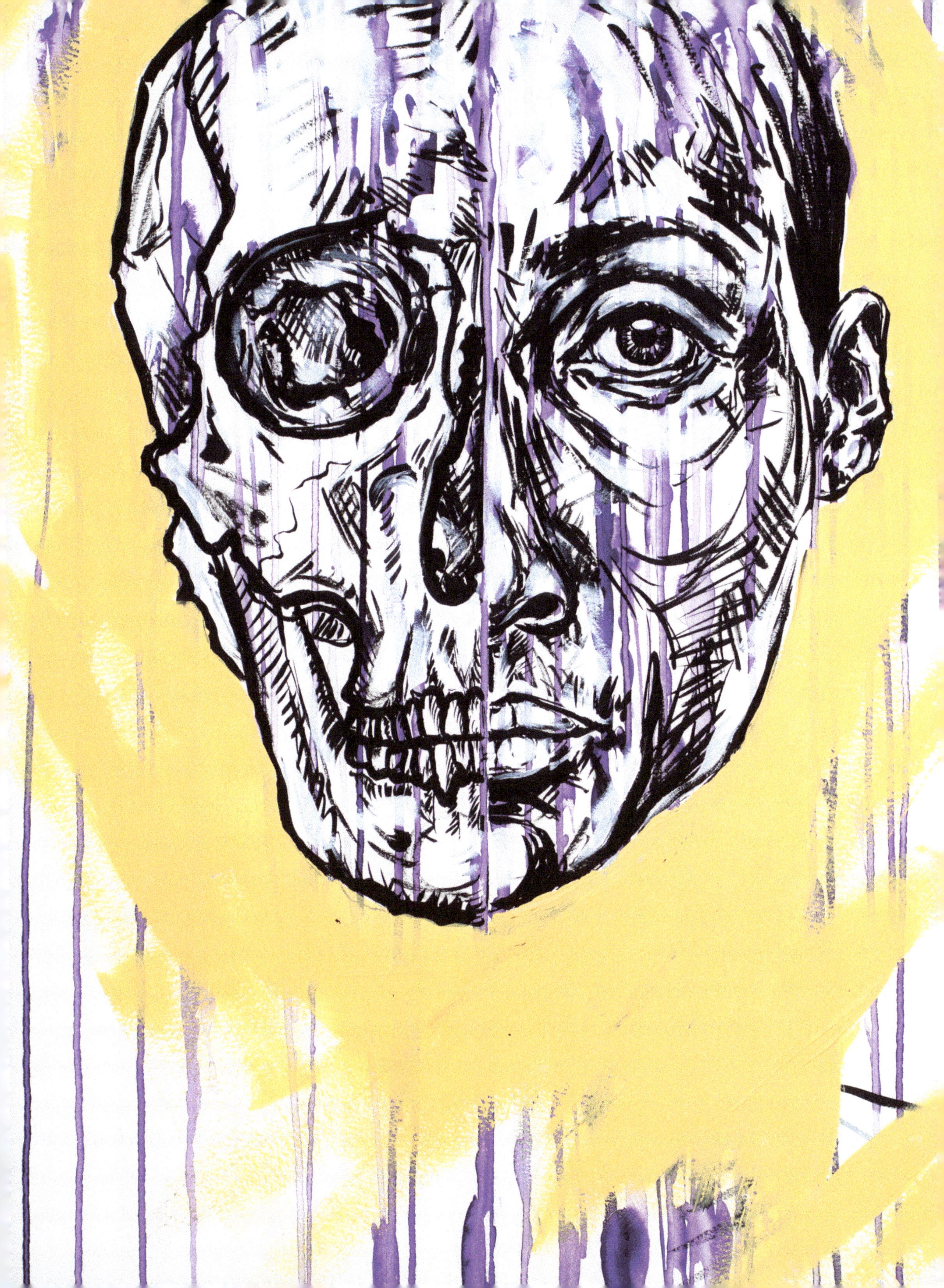

#44

EMERGE

MAY 10, 2020

I'm feeling as though I've been in this little cocoon these past few weeks, & now with the murmurings of restrictions being slowly lifted, it's like coming out of the cocoon ever so quietly, with caution. When we emerge from our isolated spaces, will we have grown? Will we be better? Will we have become internally more beautiful, just as the butterfly becomes externally? Let's emerge as we each should from our own journey, all of us different than before.

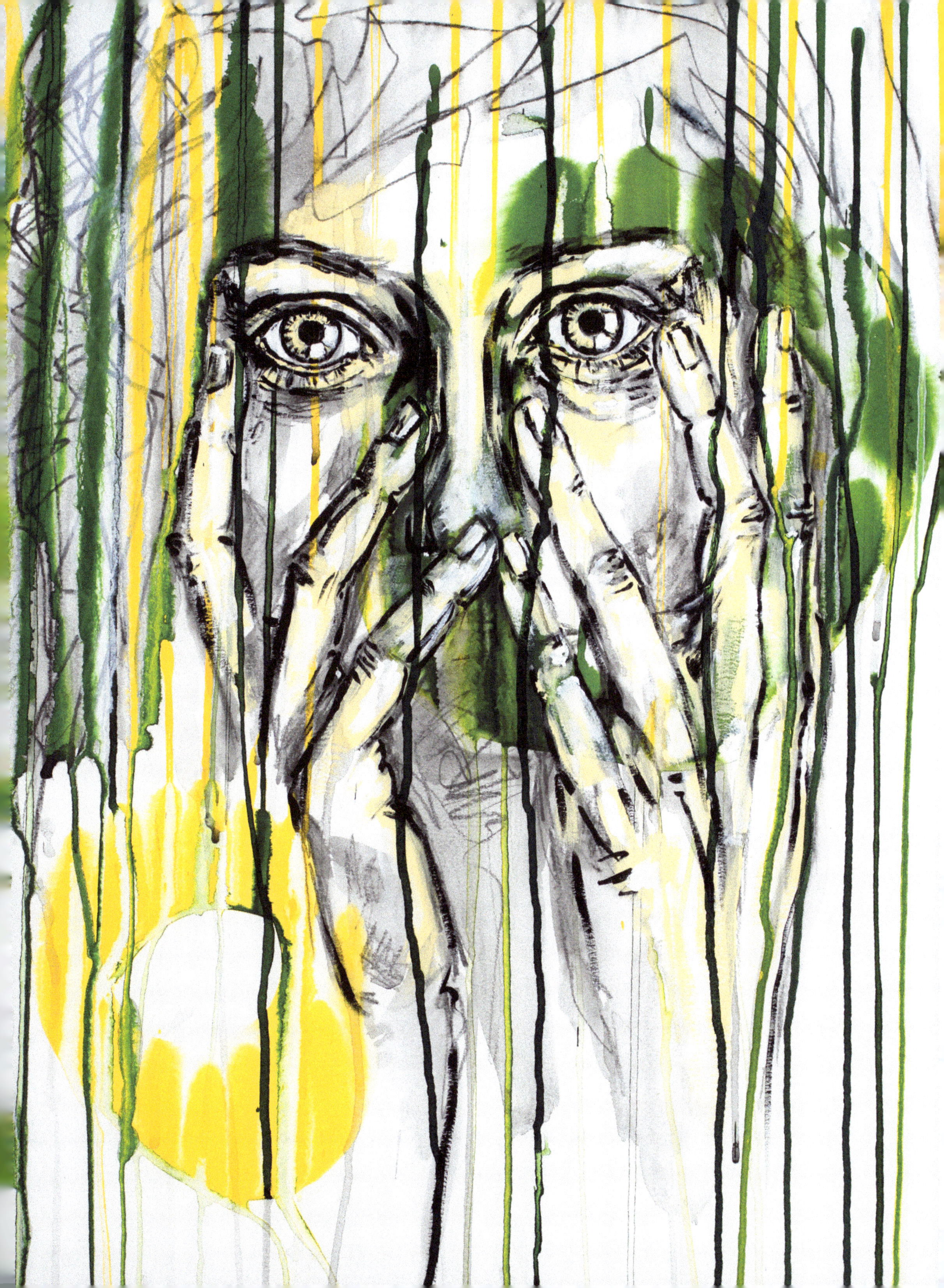

#45

TRUTH?

MAY 11, 2020

Truth as a question. I suppose that's always the case with everything, but right now more than ever before, none of us know without a doubt, the honest & FULL truth of it all. The words, explanations, theories, excuses & opinions coming out of everyone's mouths (government, experts, strangers, friends)—it's a lot—& we may never know the truth. But don't stop asking the questions & don't stop adding the question mark. . . & when the answers are silence? This speaks louder than words.

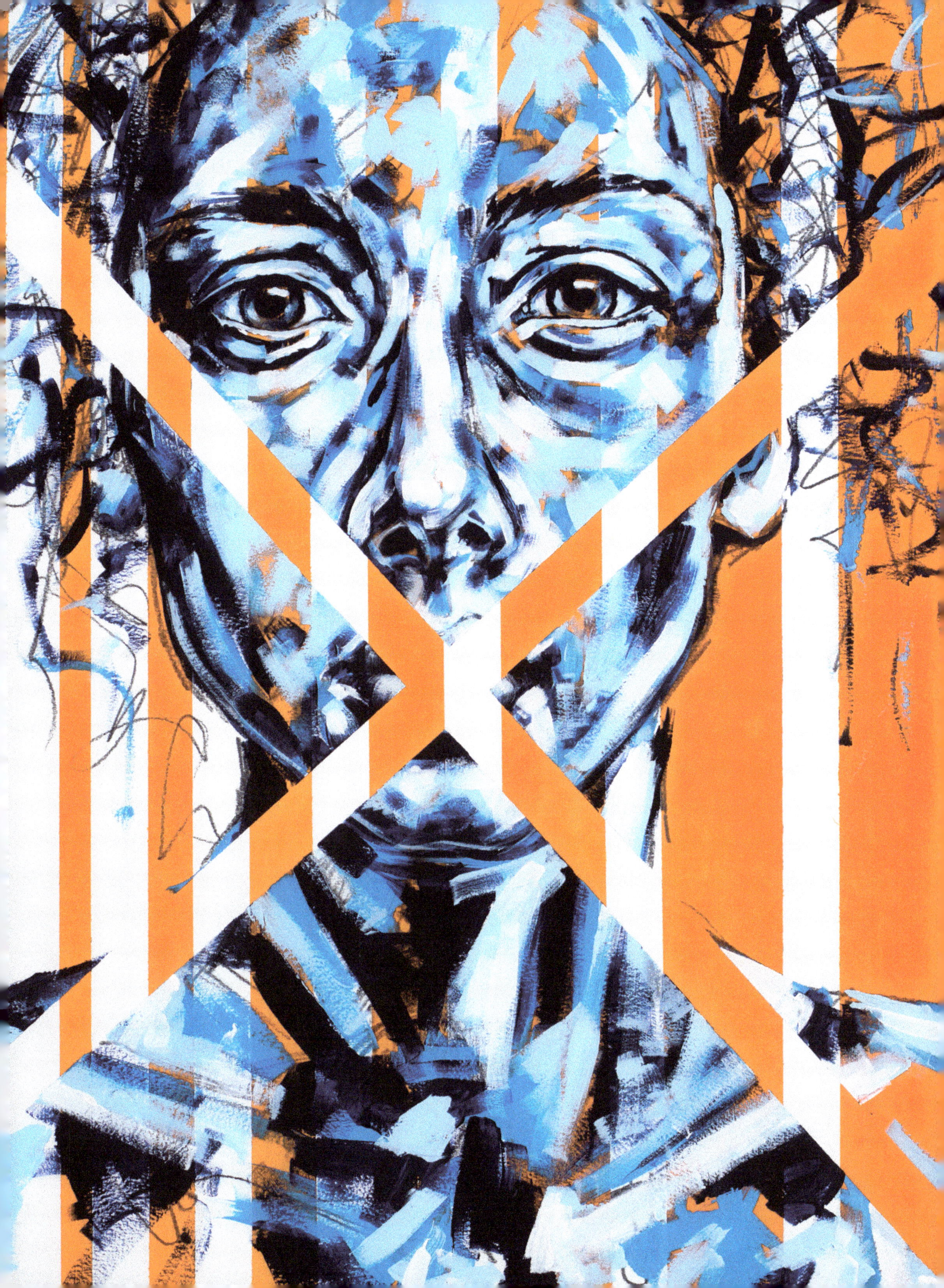

#46

DIVIDED

MAY 12, 2020

When thinking of being divided right now, my first thought goes to the general population: how it's divided between opinions about opening up everything or staying home longer. But this divide is the obvious one (it's constant & it's everywhere you look). I'm also thinking of the divide from my own perspective: some days I lean more one way & some days it's the other way. It's interesting how much influence is all around us right now. It's almost impossible not to be a little divided, even if it's not straight down the middle. What you decide, do it for yourself, do it with your gut & follow your heart.

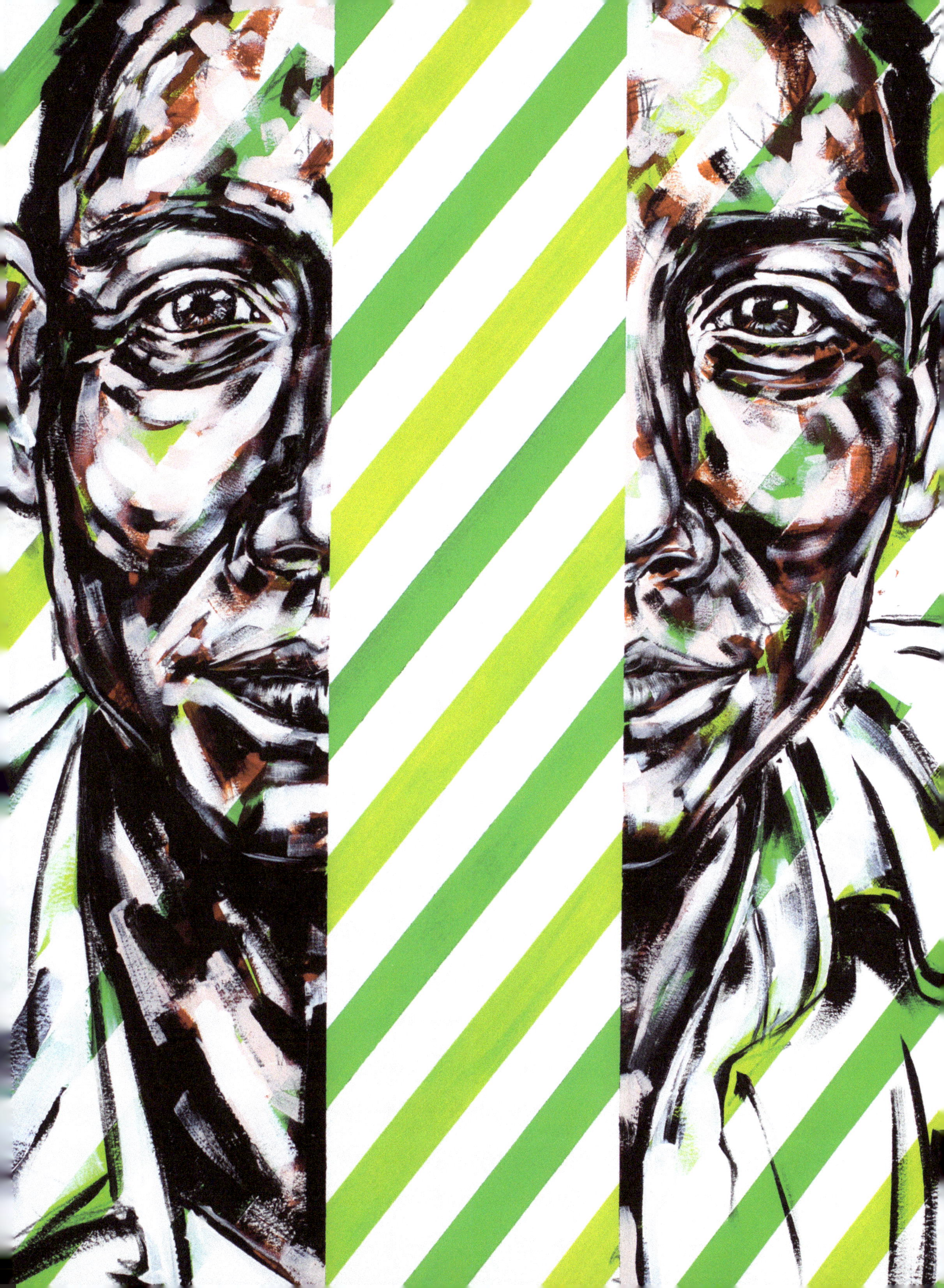

#47

WHAT?!

MAY 13, 2020

This one is my little humour/satire break. I think in these past few weeks every one of us has said, "what?!" more than once. I mean, what else can you say? Unimaginable things have been happening & what's that old saying, "if you don't laugh, you'll cry"? I think we should all take a moment today, to yell, "WHAT?!" & then have a good laugh. It'll be good for the soul.

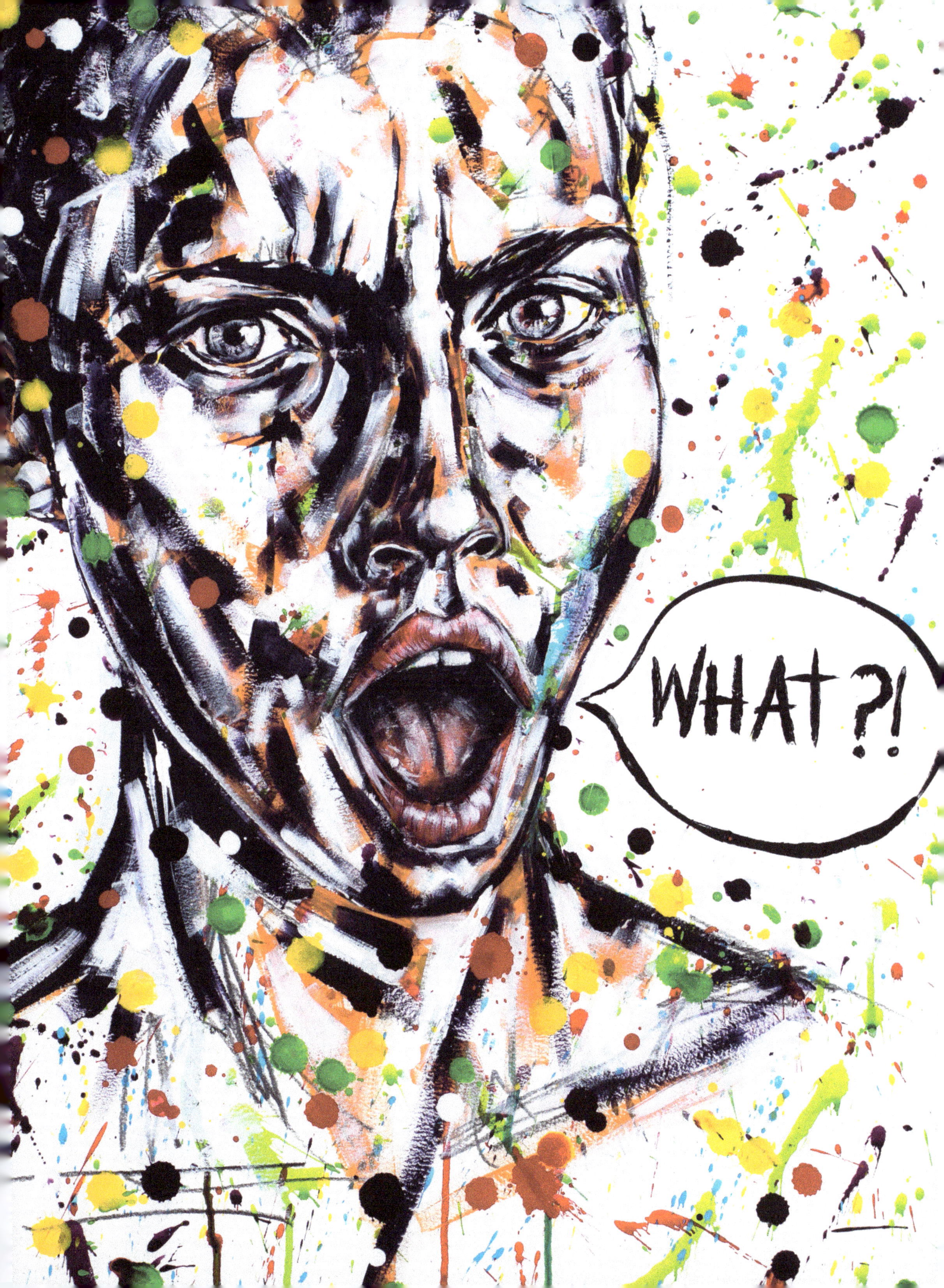
WHAT?!

#48

PLACID

MAY 14, 2020

Does it feel like after living through phase one of this pandemic, that a couple of months ago we all thought would be impossible, & nothing else could really surprise us? Aside from an alien invasion happening, we have adapted with a degree of "cool" that is rivalled only by The Fonz. What could they say that would shock us now? First it was Trump becoming president & now a virus that shut down the whole world. Surprises will be more like a tiny hole with a slow leak instead of balloons popping.

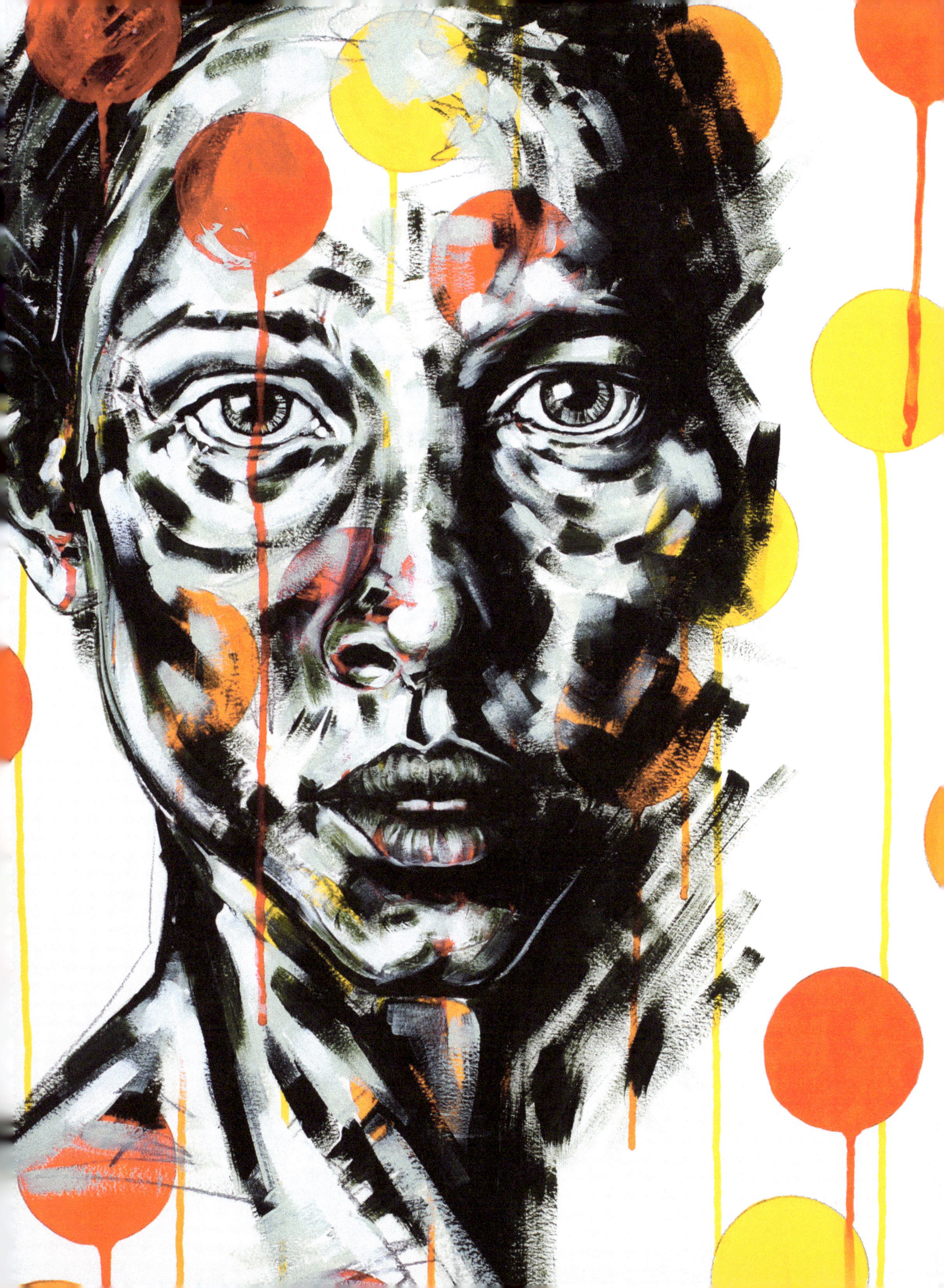

#49

INVISIBLE

MAY 15, 2020

Remember when you were a kid, playing outside? Maybe it was kick the can or some other adventure game? If you smeared mud on your face, not only did you feel kind of like a badass, you felt invisible to the opponent—without a doubt, they couldn't catch you. I was thinking about the masks we most likely will all be required to wear. Whether you agree with it or not, how are they going to make us feel? Invincible? Or just invisible? Health & self-care first, of course, but maybe some war paint might not be a bad idea, too.

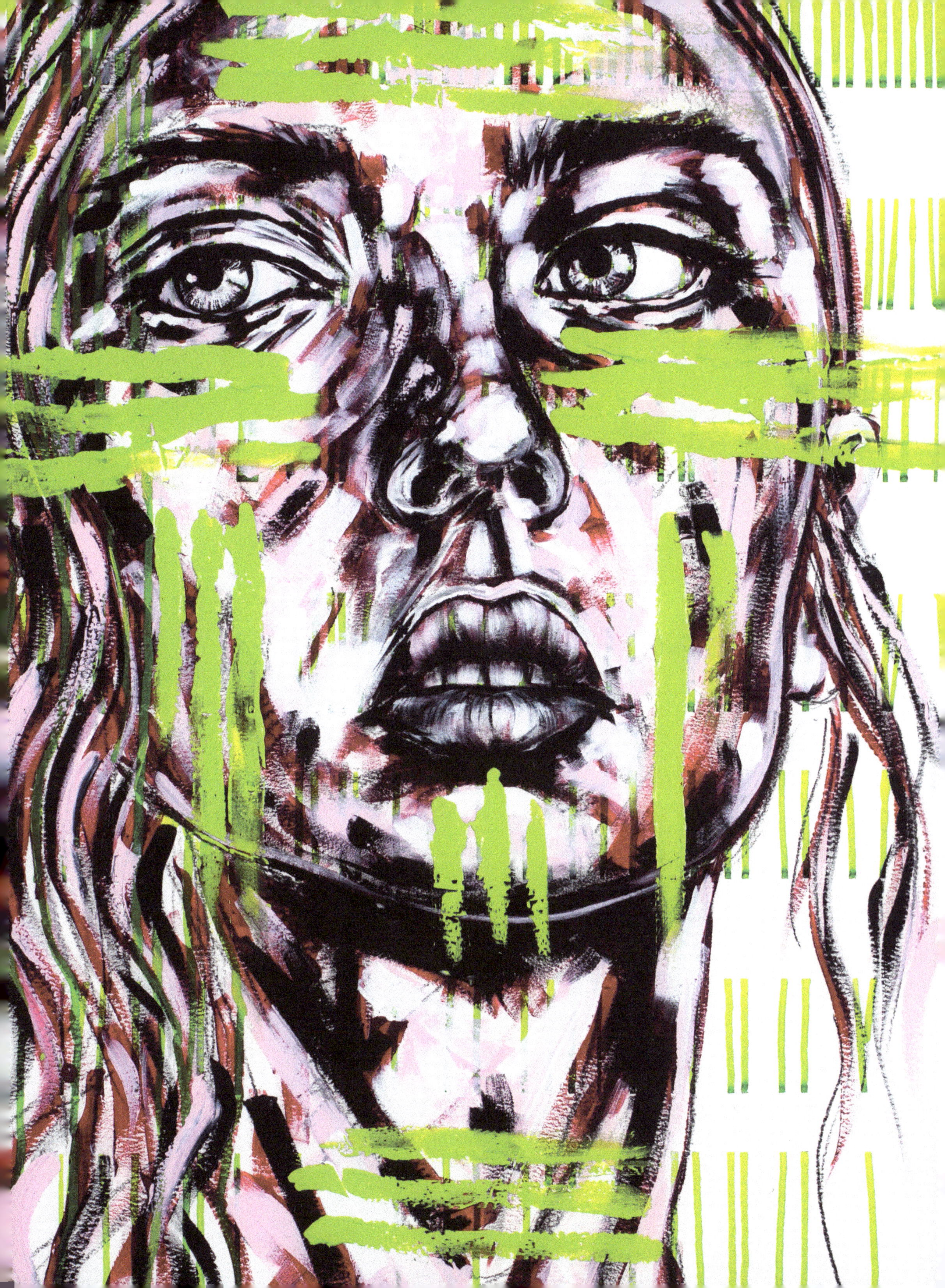

#50

NOISE

MAY 16, 2020

Too much. . . too much noise about everything all over the place, with no clarity. Things are now starting to open & I don't think anyone has a clear idea of what to do, when they should do it, or how they should feel about it. The noise is too much (literal or not). I think I'd like to pull from the recently (& very unfortunately) deceased comedic legend, Jerry Stiller & his character Frank Costanza, & yell, "SERENITY NOW!" The noise needs to be let go of, so we can make decisions while quietly looking within.

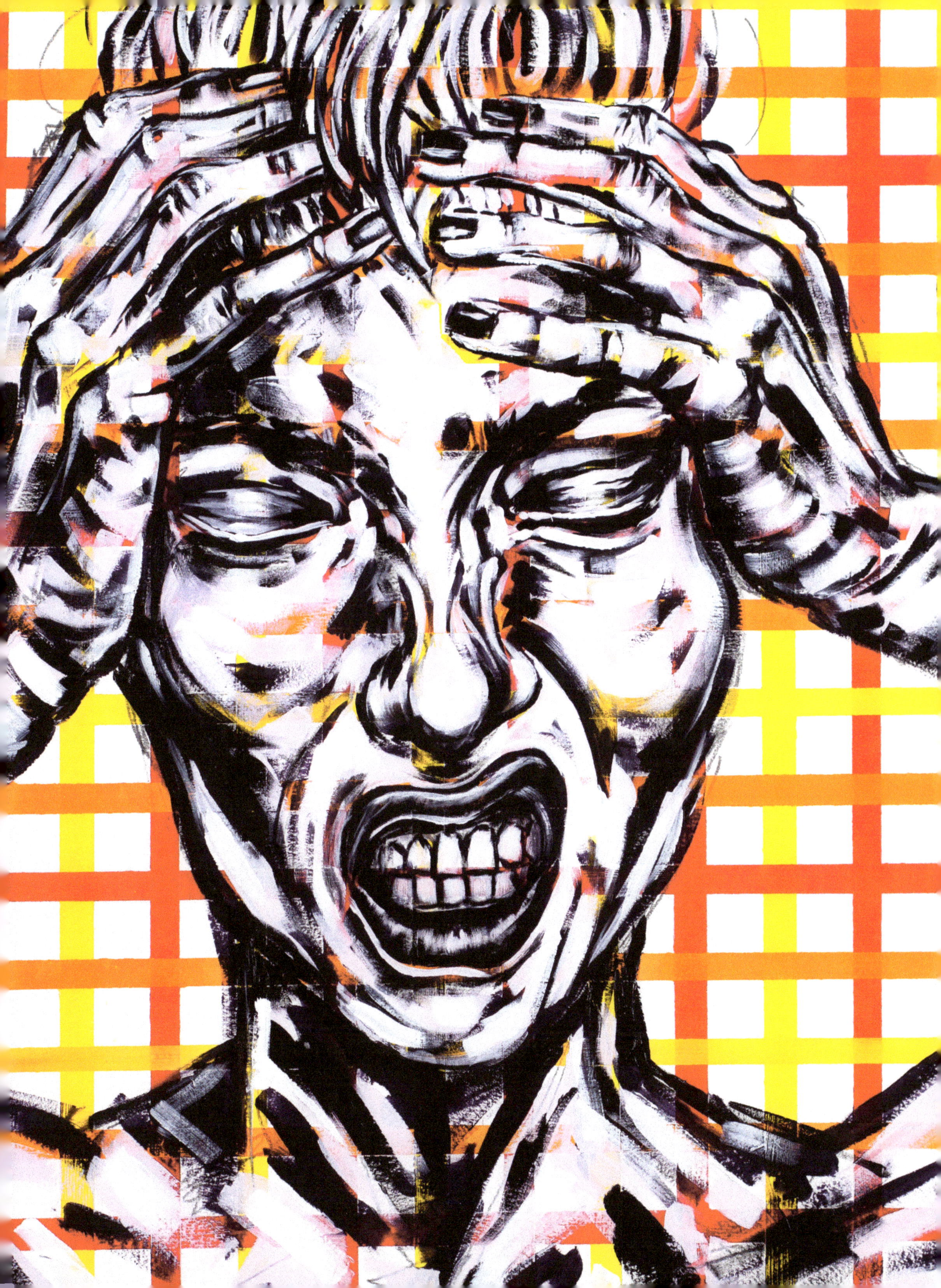

#51

CONTEMPLATE

MAY 17, 2020

To look at or view with continued attention; observe or study thoughtfully. Contemplating what my life was like before the pandemic vs. during vs. afterwards & really looking at it thoughtfully. What patterns repeated or disappeared? Which actions will resurface? How will my new routine fit with resurfacing to the socially acceptable normal? What do I want to return to & what should I leave in the past completely? Contemplation is powerful so use it to move forward with grace & intention.

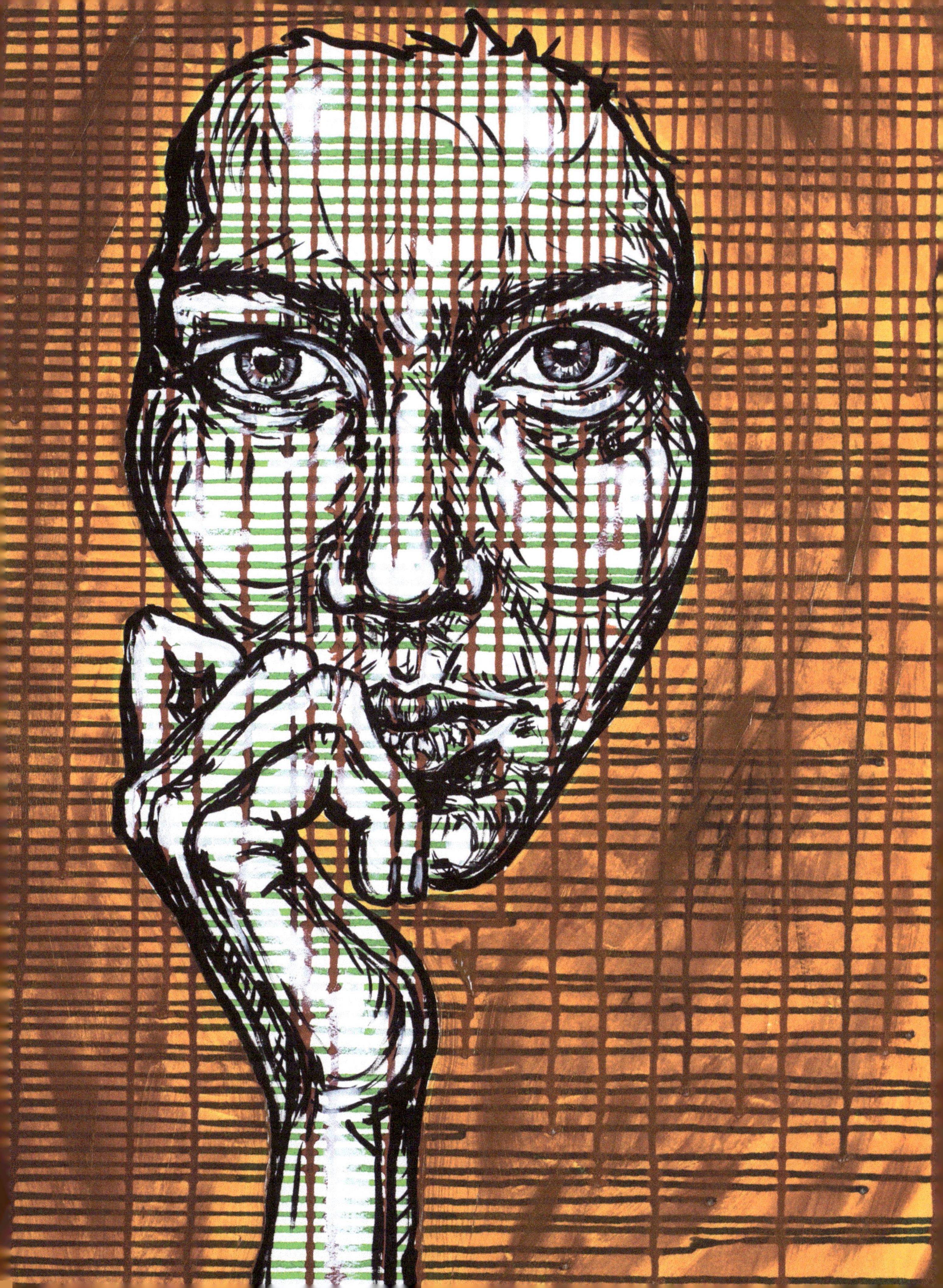

#52

FRAGMENT

MAY 18, 2020

To break, to be fragmented. . . a small piece off a larger whole. Sounds a bit daunting, but seemingly necessary. Think about anything you've accomplished—isn't it usually when you break away from the pack & take a risk? I think that we've all just "fragmented" individually & as a society taken a break from the norm. Now we're preparing to put the fragments back together, so let's just make sure we put them back in the correct spots.

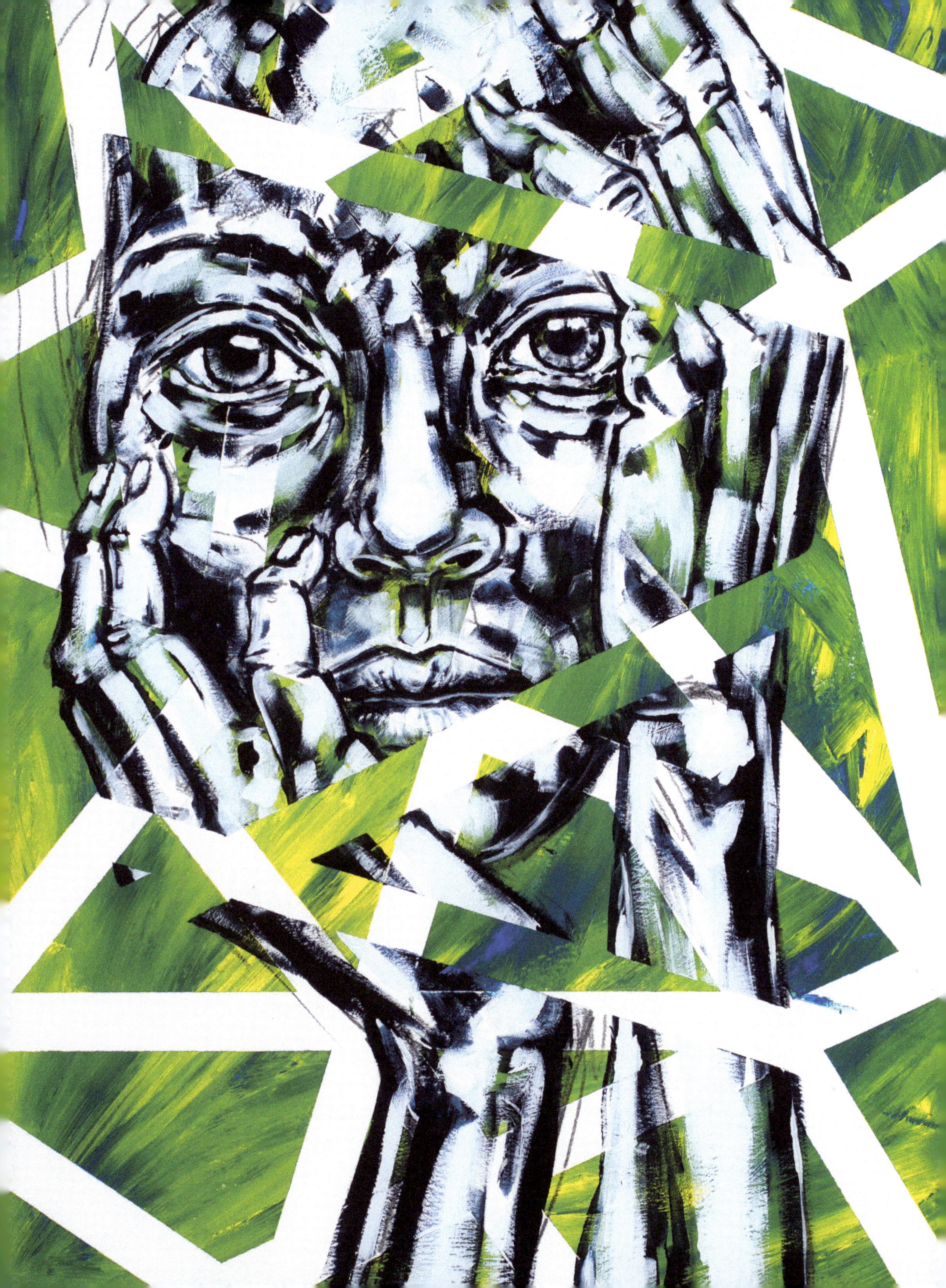

#53

ALMOST

MAY 19, 2020

Almost ready for the full-on swan dive back into reality. . . almost.

Today I did a little thing that I haven't done in over 2 months: I bought my favourite coffee beans from my favourite coffee shop. Honestly, it felt amazing! And it's such a small thing. The joys in life are big & small. I hope that I never take any of them for granted again & remember how much some beans made me smile today.

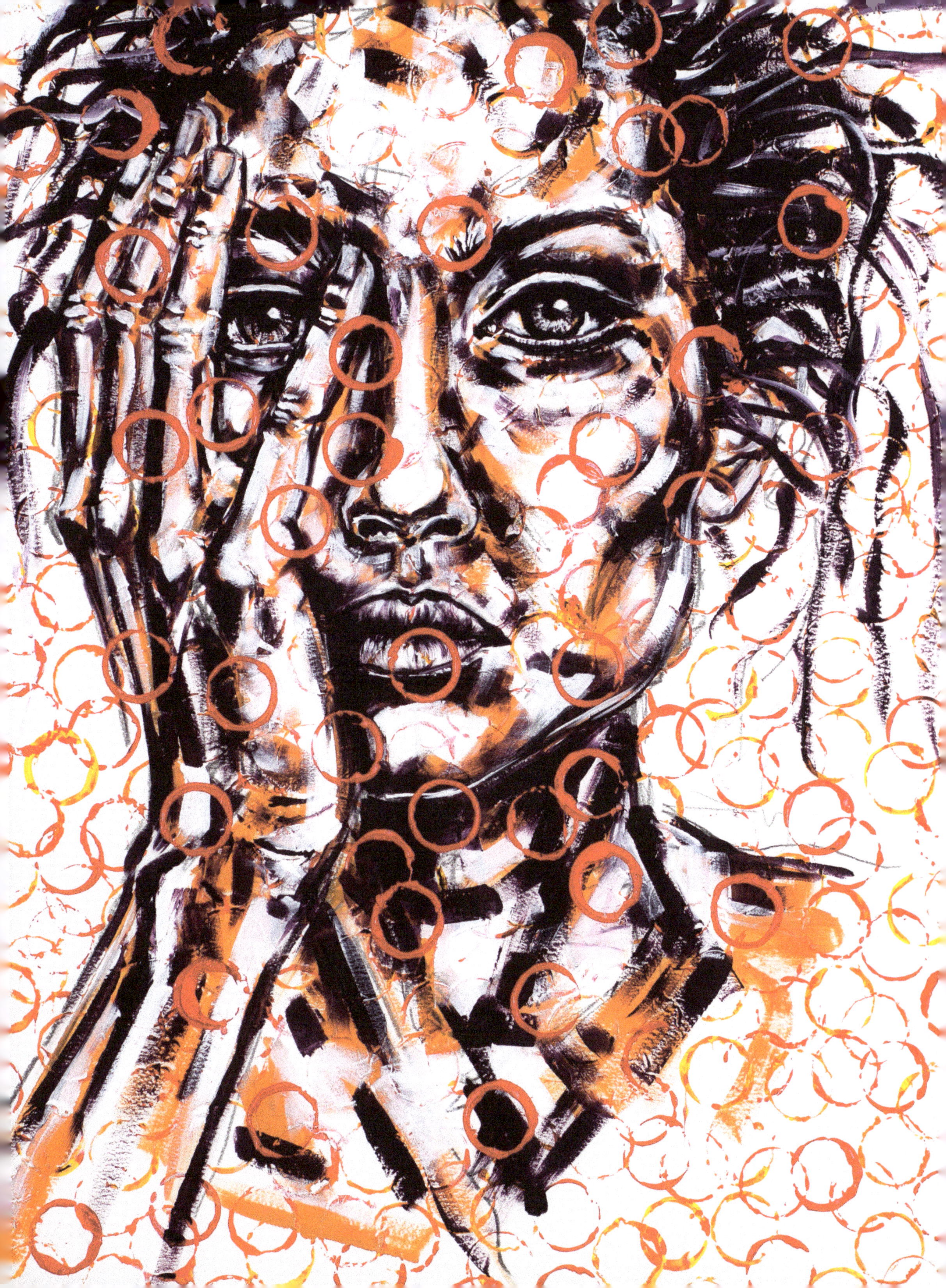

#54

PERIPHERAL

MAY 20, 2020

Relating to or situated on the edge or periphery of something. Aren't we all on edge, but also on THE edge? The return to things & people is in our peripheral vision—it's right there—or is it? Anything out of the corner of our eye is blurry & on the edge of becoming clear. Maybe when the clarity comes it won't be what we expect, but maybe it's a NEW CLARITY that we should be hoping for.

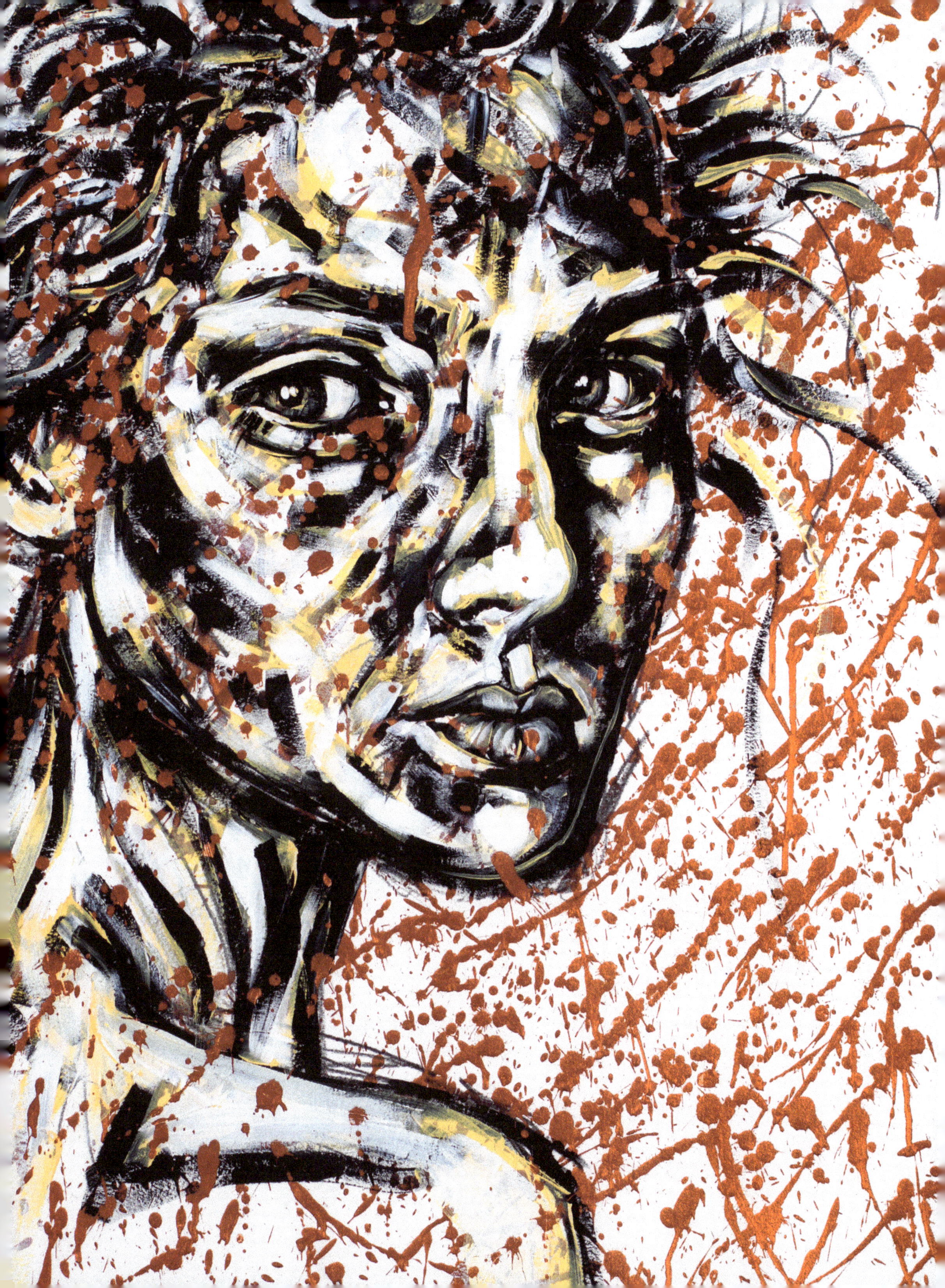

#55

MIXED

MAY 21, 2020

Yikes, I'm all over the place—thoughts, views, emotions—& it's probably because I go back to work tomorrow after 67 days off. I don't know what to expect, or how to feel about it. I'm jumping back & forth, all mixed up: from looking forward to seeing people & being social, to feeling apprehensive &—to be honest—a little disheartened, & I'm not even sure why. It's emotional chaos over here, but just like we adapted to the shutdown, we'll adapt to everything else. In the meantime, I'm going to chill & enjoy the rest of today.

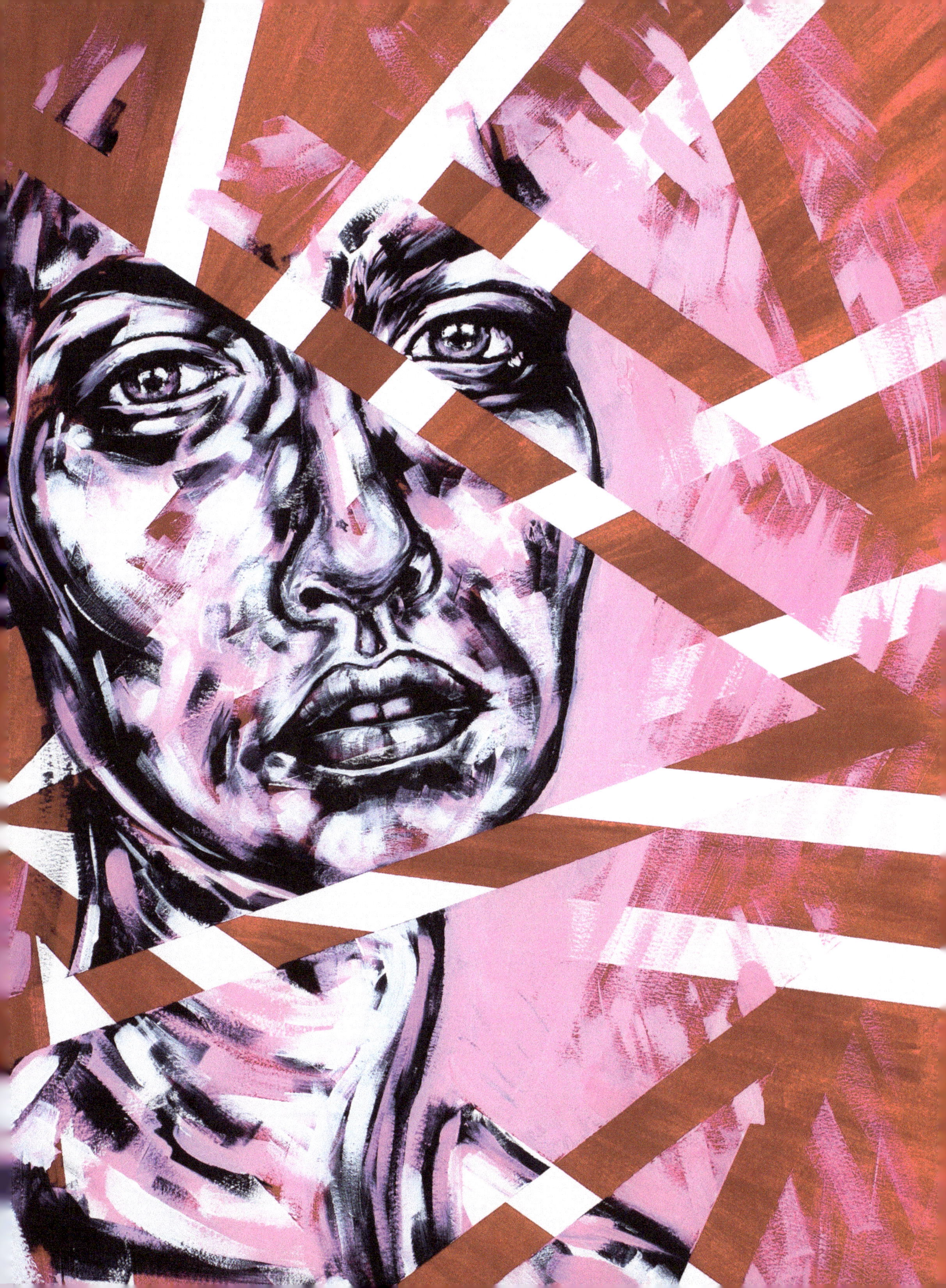

#56

CONTENT

MAY 22, 2020

Can we be content with the new normal, which is just constant changes? I guess that'll be what keeps us all on our toes. I'm practicing being content with life, & appreciating each day. I'm grateful to live in the country that I do. And after my first day back at work, a little side note: if you go out to restaurants (or anywhere really), please be content with just being out. Be patient with everyone who is working, as kinks will have to be ironed out, & your kindness will be appreciated.

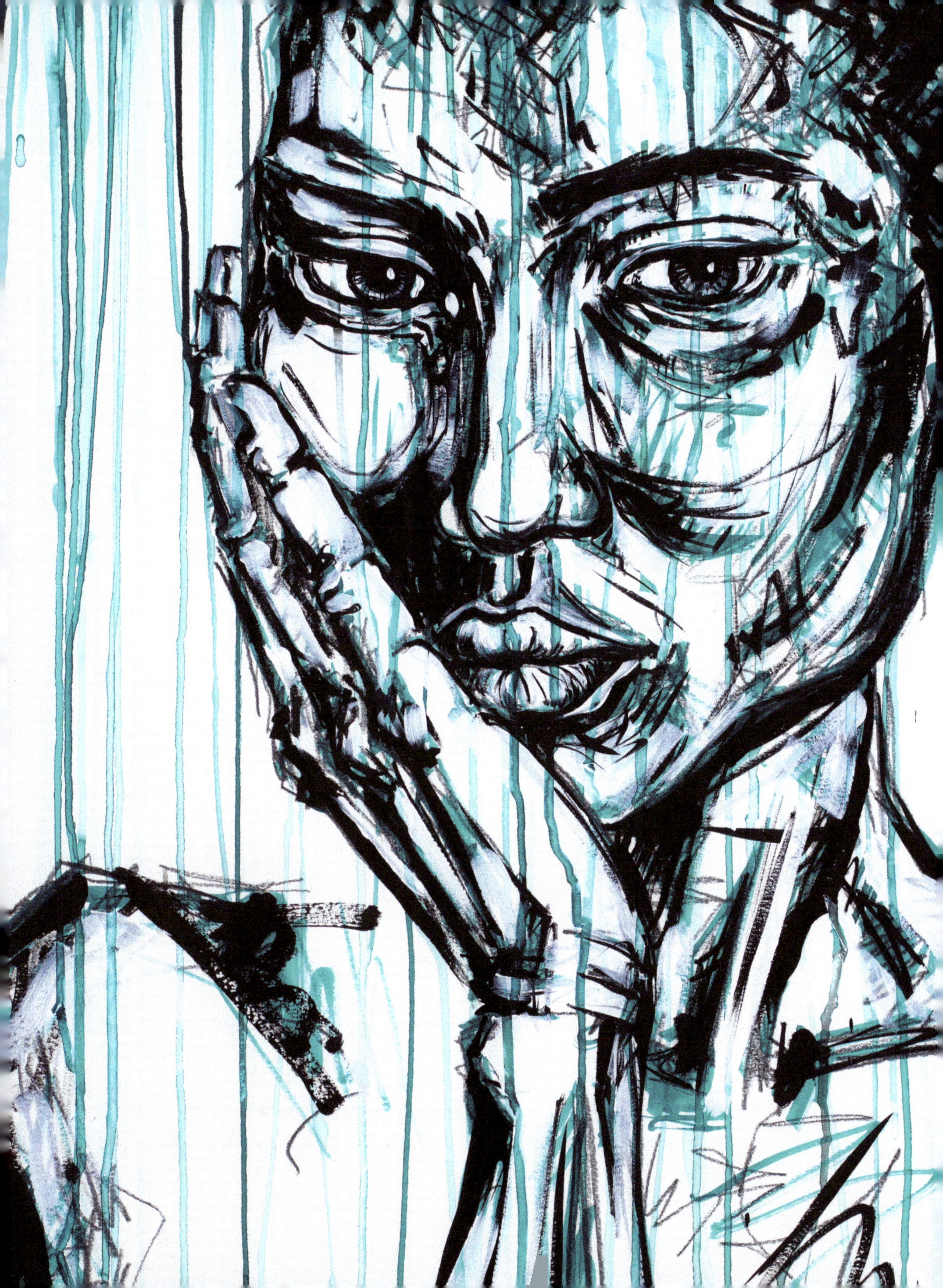

#57

OBSCURE

MAY 23, 2020

Uncertainty, obscurity, reality being concealed? Yes! I've been back at work for 2 days & it's a little like I never left & a little like everything has changed. It's awkward—all my observations are odd. I will say this: people missed social interactions massively. The need to be social is outweighing the fear of the virus, at least in my work environment. Who knows what is right or what will happen, but yes, obscure is the word for work—at least for right now.

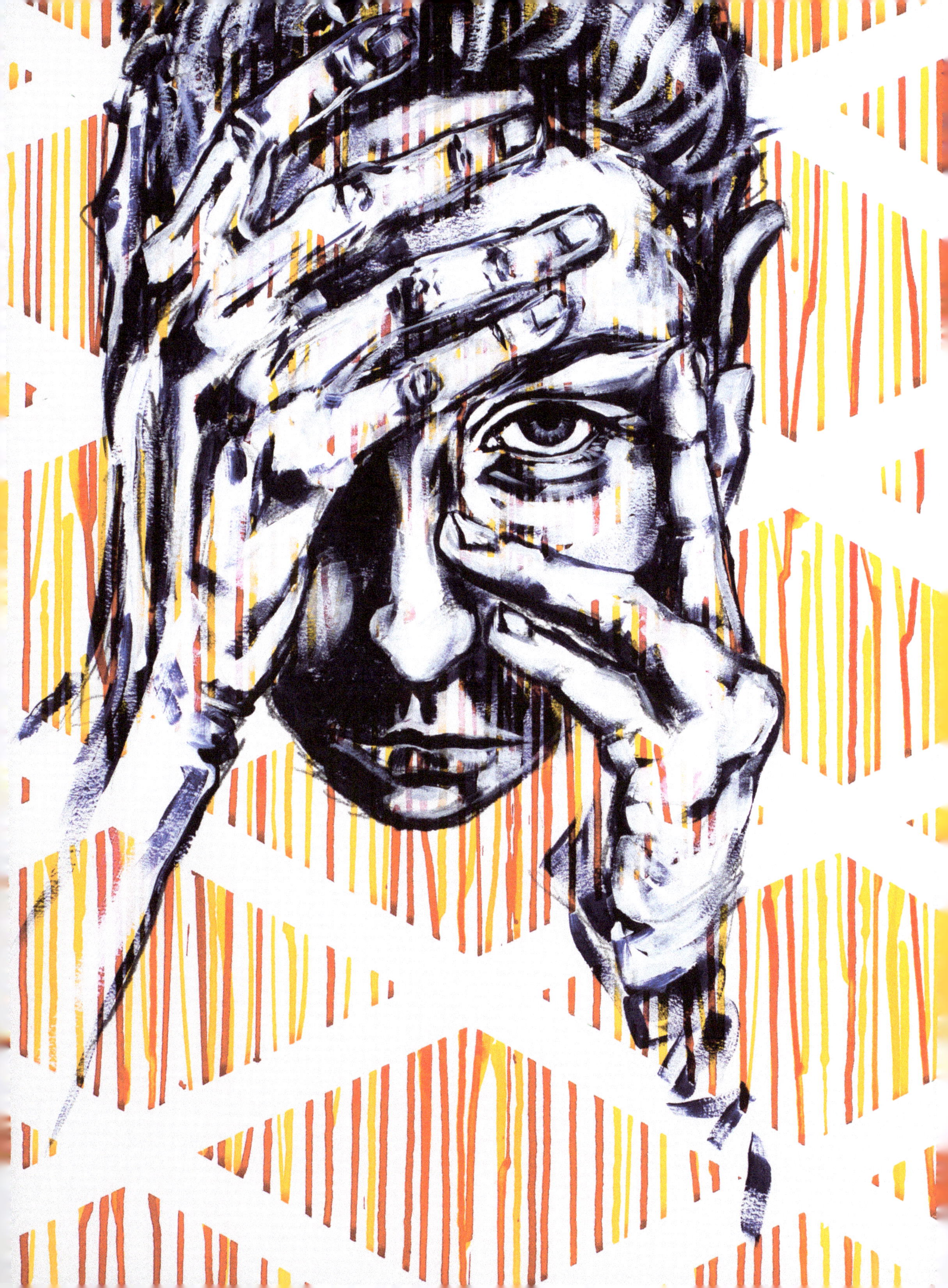

#58

TIRED

MAY 24, 2020

Wowza! Being away from people for over 2 months, I'm now 3 days in & I'm exhausted. It's crazy. The amount of energy you use when dealing with the public is a lot! I'm in the service industry & of course this is true for so many jobs, so, kudos to all the people dealing with people!! Smiles & laughter are the only way to go! Spread the love everyone.

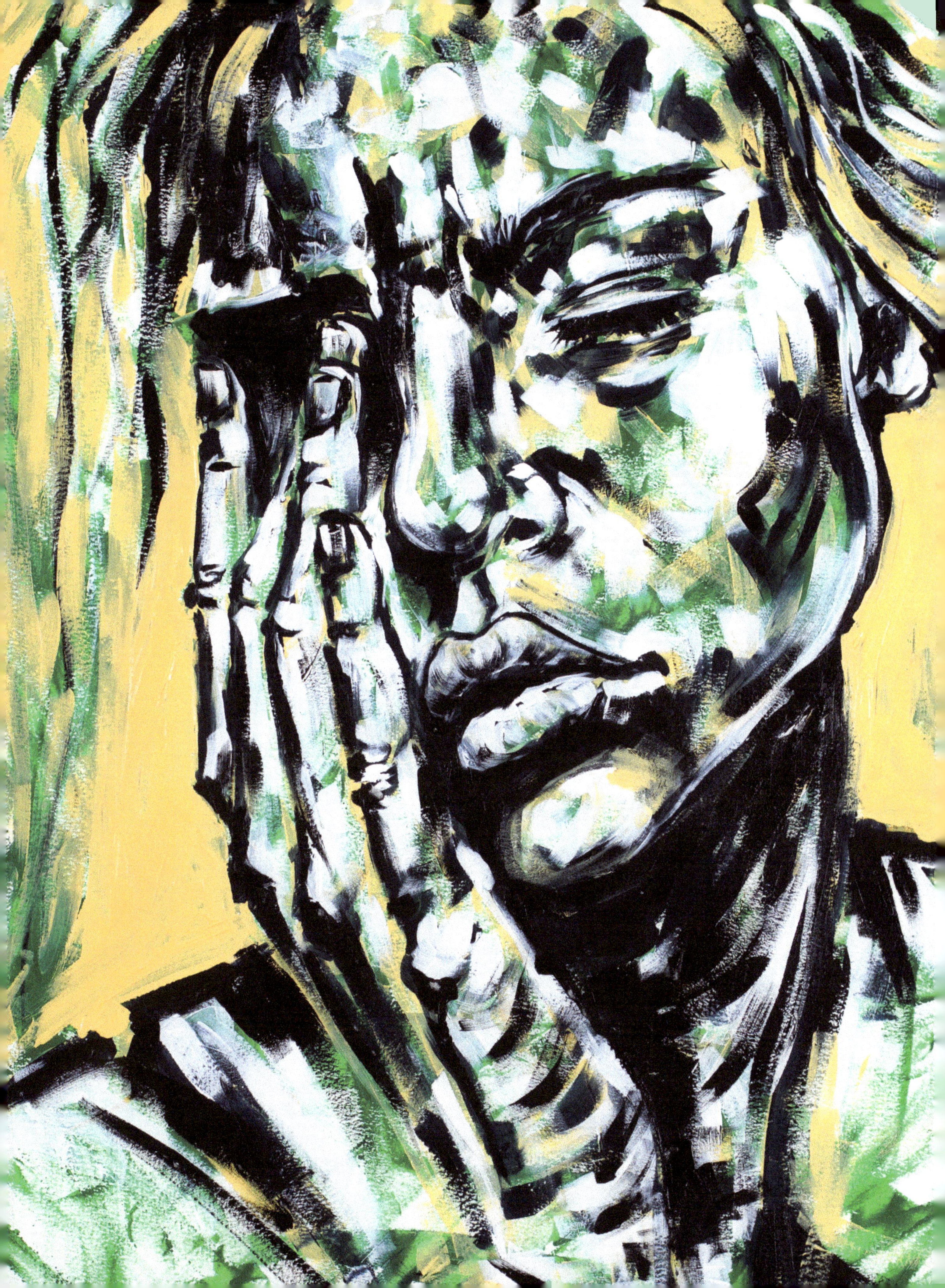

#59

ANNOYED

MAY 25, 2020

I really hope that the things we learnt during the shutdown will be remembered & brought with us, during this re-entry back into public spaces & environments. The priorities we talked about, the grace & patience we said we learnt are important, let's not jump back in with both feet while also blindfolded. Let's be thoughtful & mindful. What we just went through can't be meaningless. This part is up to each of us.

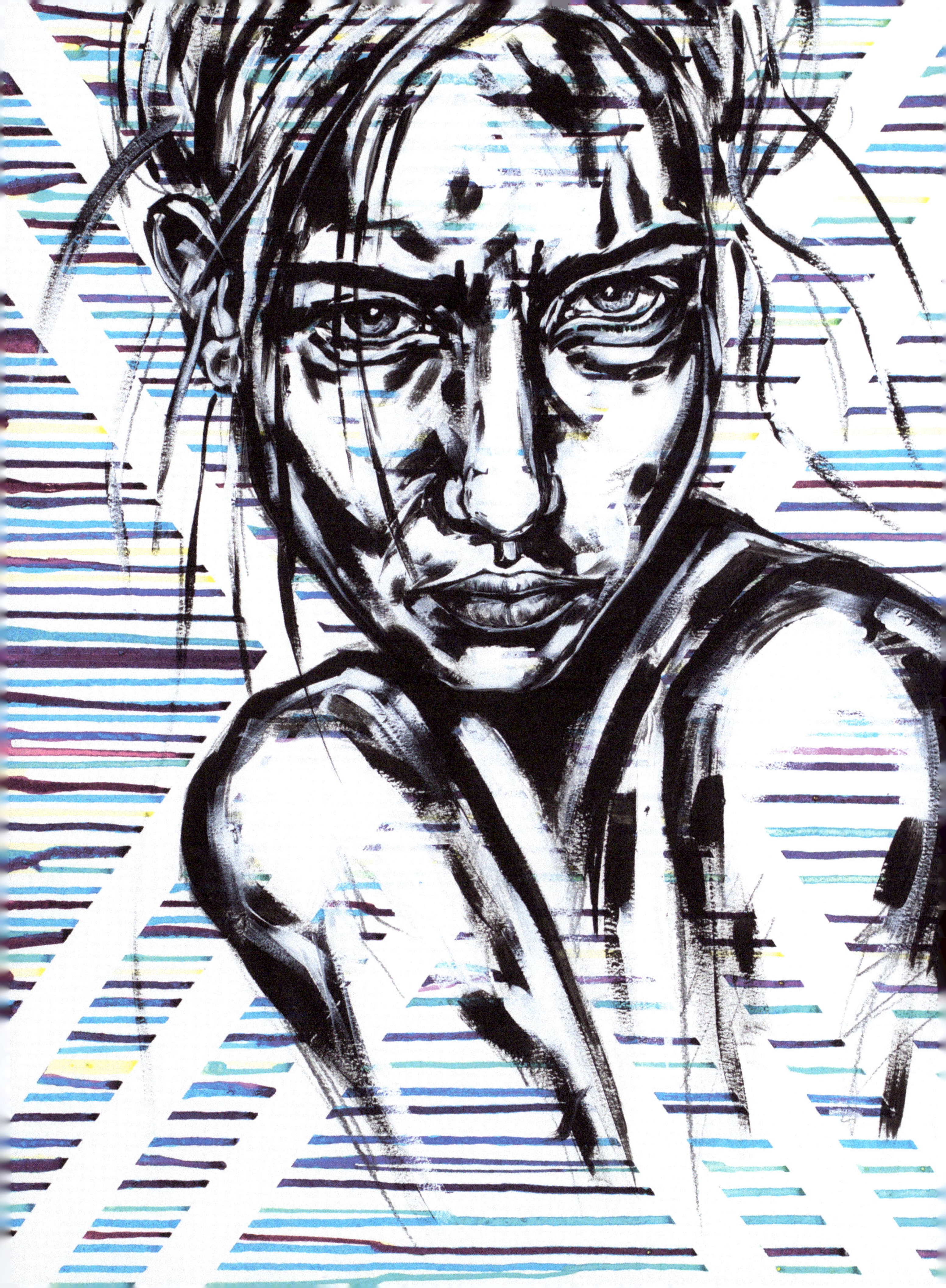

#60

MIC DROP

MAY 26, 2020

As we all figure out this next chapter of a never-before-read book, I am ending the series that got me through the first chapter—it's time to move forward. What started as just a little challenge for myself to paint every day, ended in a huge personal journey of growth, & an experience that connected me to so many. I am so unbelievably grateful to everyone for their kind words, support & encouragement: it's been humbling & amazing. So with this last piece of the *Pandemic* series, I say a profoundly heartfelt THANK YOU!

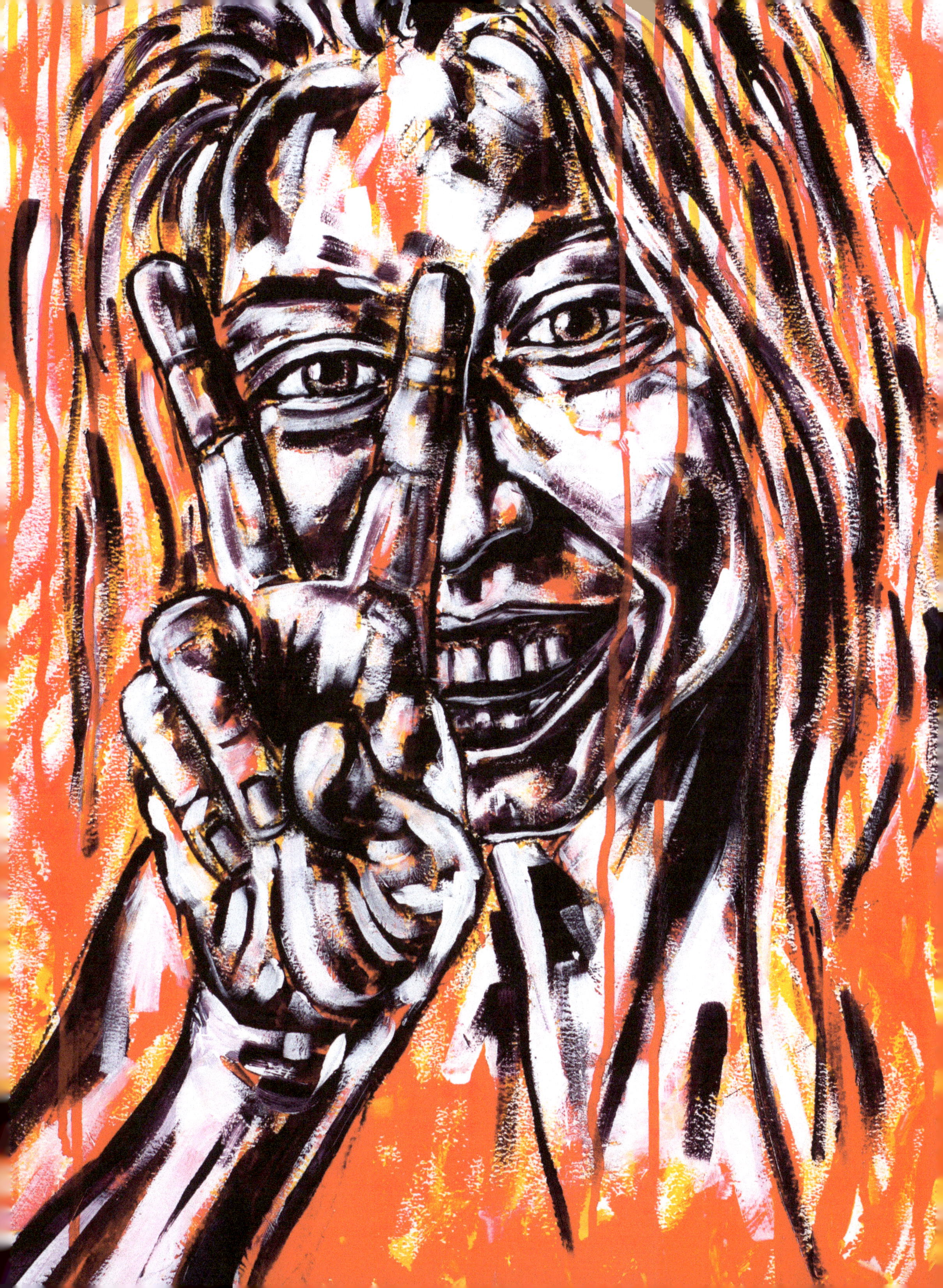

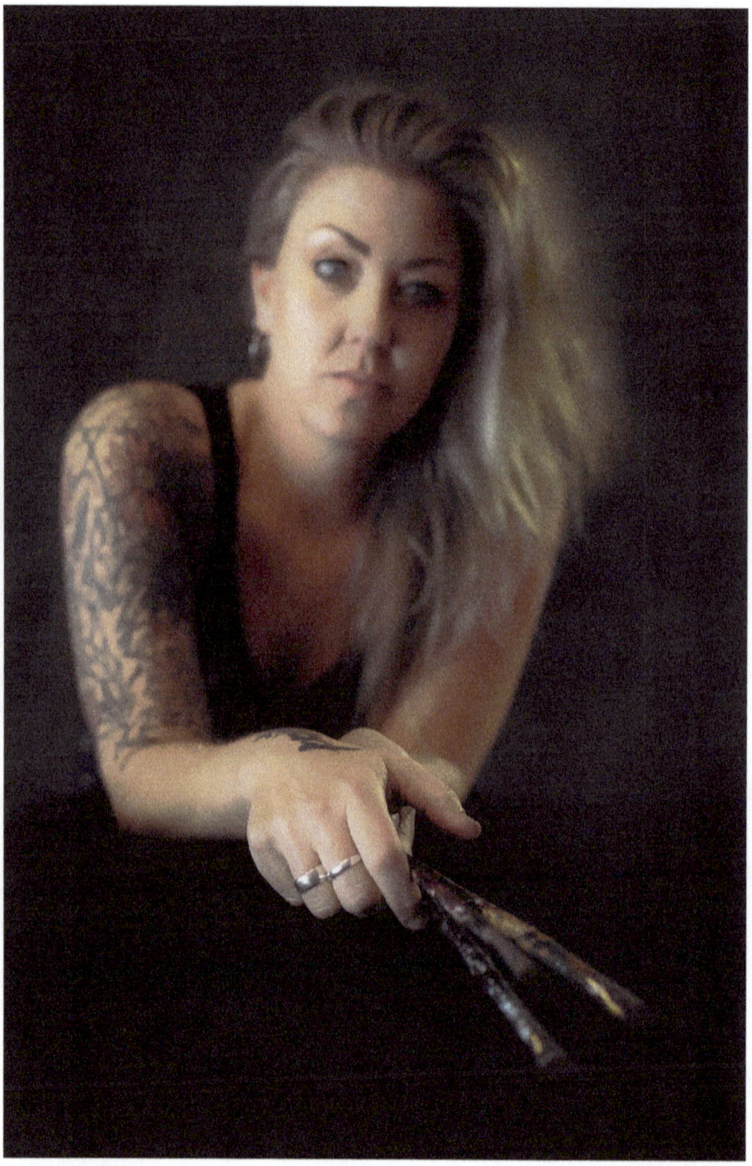

ABOUT THE ARTIST

Melissa Dinwoodie is a visual artist living in Kelowna, British Columbia, Canada. She specializes in acrylic and mixed media painting and illustration. Her practice focuses on figurative and portrait art. She is fascinated with the possible connection between the viewer and subject matter.

Always experimenting with different materials and surfaces, Melissa believes that art can be the connection between people that encourages conversations, relationships, education and growth. The art process is her survival guide and the way she connects.

To view more work and connect:
melissadinwoodie.com
Instagram: @melissadinwoodieart

A special thank you to my best friend, the other Melissa.
All photography by vothphotography.com